T0104116

PHYSICS

for Curious Kids

An illustrated introduction to energy, matter, forces, and our Universe!

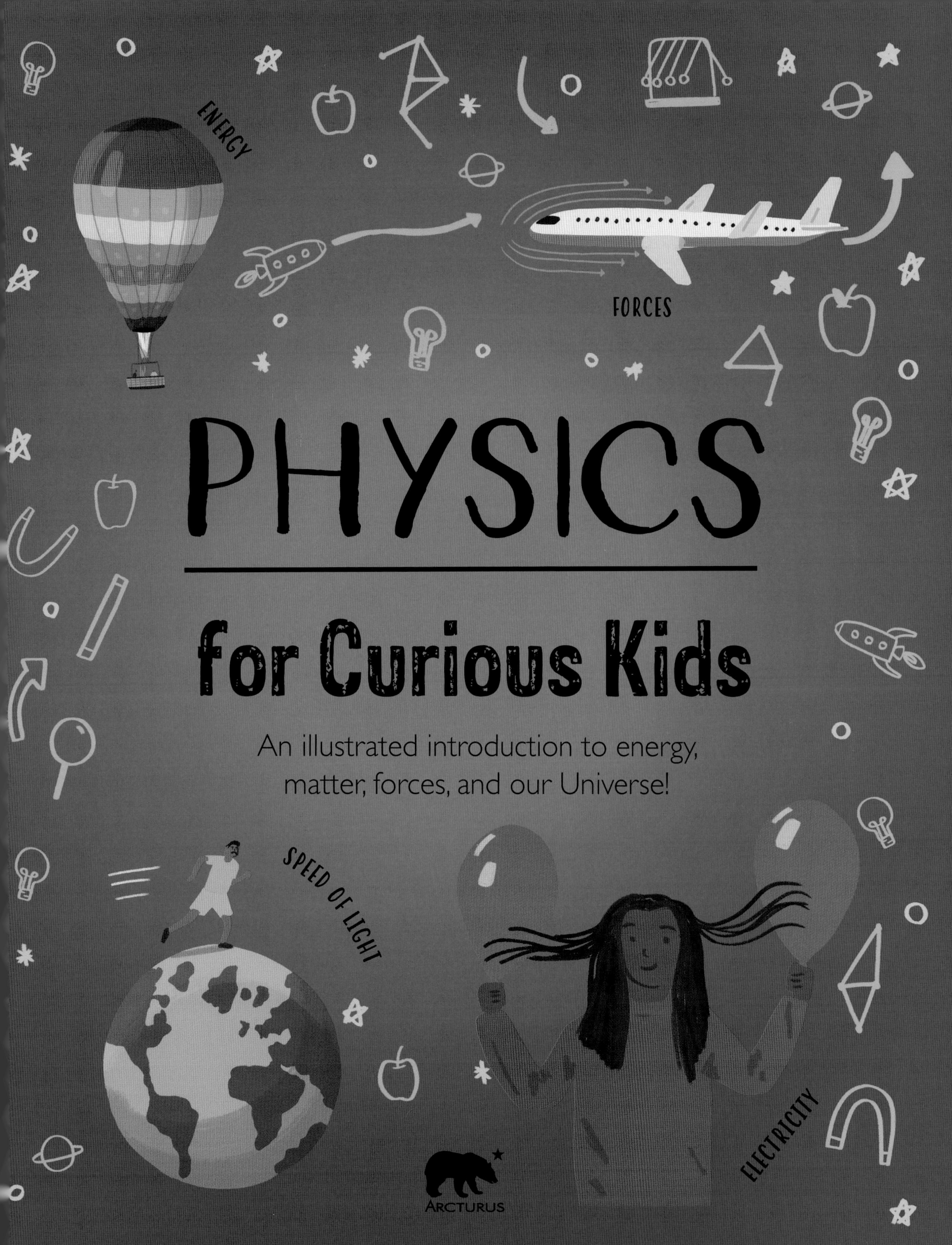

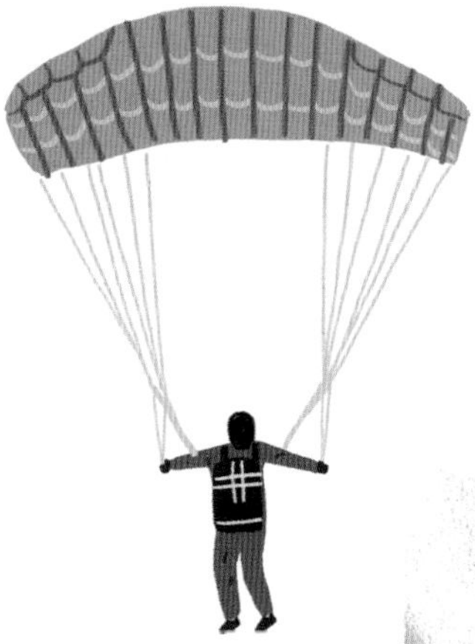

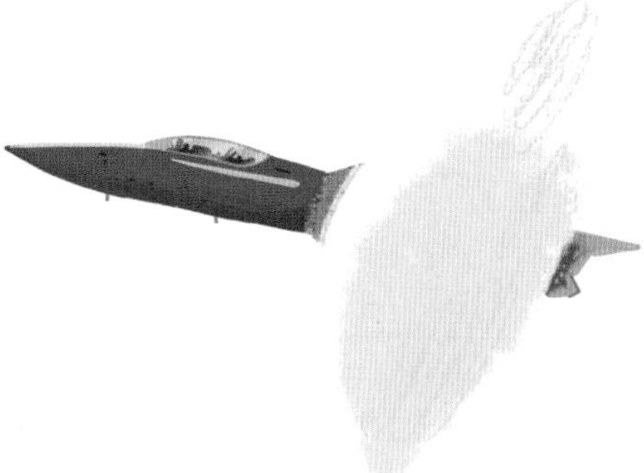

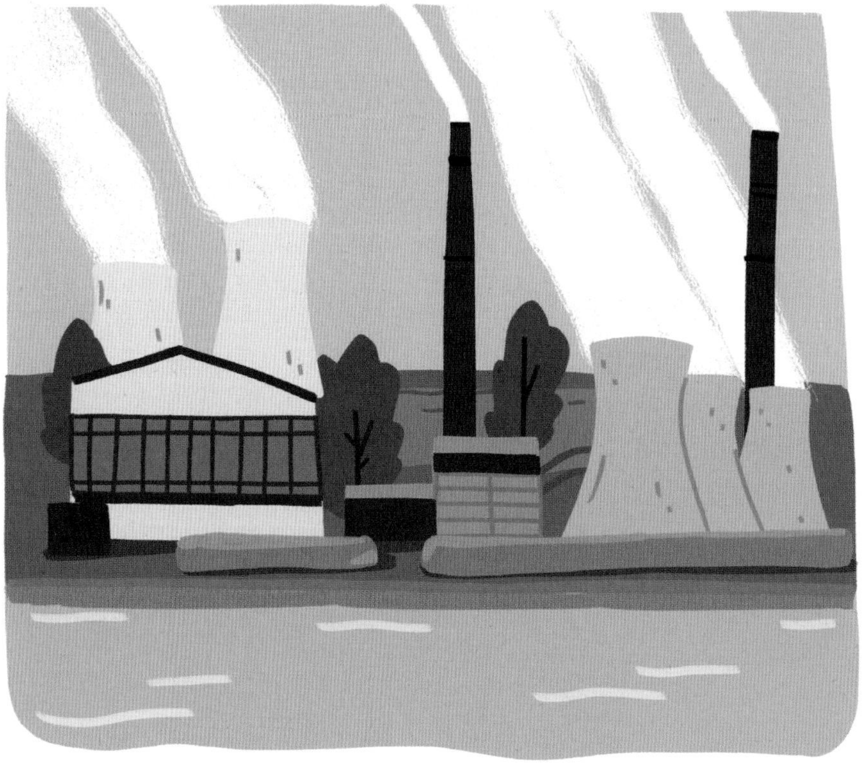

This edition published in 2024 by Arcturus Publishing Limited
26/27 Bickels Yard, 151–153 Bermondsey Street,
London SE1 3HA

Author: Laura Baker
Illustrator: Alex Foster
Consultant: Anne Rooney
Designer: Jeanette Ryall
Packaged by Cloud King Creative

ISBN: 978-1-3988-0387-9
CH008271US
Supplier 29, Date 1023, PI 00005650

Printed in China

What is STEM?

STEM is a world-wide initiative that aims to cultivate an interest in Science, Technology, Engineering, and Mathematics, in an effort to promote these disciplines to as wide a variety of students as possible.

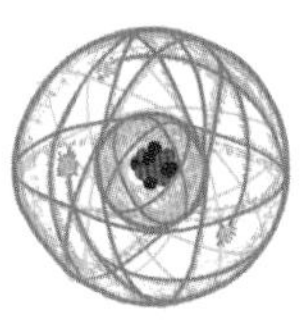

CONTENTS

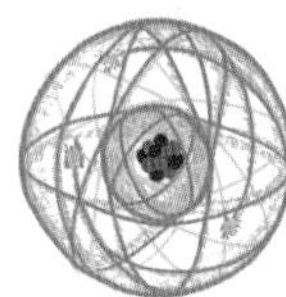

WELCOME TO FASCINATING PHYSICS

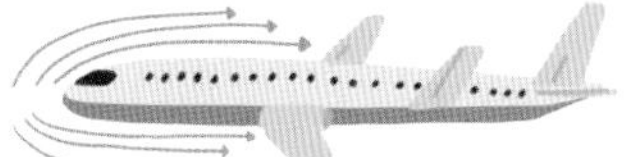

The earth-shaking blast of a rocket launching. The mysterious click of magnets coming together. The unbelievable heights of a bridge suspended over water. The light that helps us see. All of these have something in common. They can all be explained by **physics**.

Physics is the study of energy and matter and how they relate to each other in space and time. Physics can be as small as atoms or as big as the Universe! Some people look closely at the laws and forces of physics—for them it's all about the action! For others, it's about understanding how waves can make light and sound. Yet others look at energy, electricity, and even space.

The people who study physics are called **physicists**. They strive to understand how our great big Universe, and everything inside it, behaves.

Become a physicist yourself as you flip through these pages and discover mind-bending, fascinating facts about the world around you.

THINK LIKE A PHYSICIST

Physics is a branch of **science.** Science is all about understanding our world and the great big Universe. As we discover more about our magnificent planet, we also come across more questions. By continuing to seek answers and explanations, we can learn and grow. Science can even help us live better lives. So how do we think like physicists?

QUESTION EVERYTHING

A big part of being a scientist is asking questions. If a scientist doesn't understand something, they ask a question. They then make **predictions** and form a **hypothesis** about what the answer might be. A hypothesis is a suggested explanation that gives a starting point to investigate.

Scientists then design **experiments** to test their hypothesis, make observations, or gather data. They ensure that the conditions of the experiment can stay the same and that the result can be repeated. It may take many attempts for the experiment to work and a **conclusion** to be drawn. Thomas Edison made hundreds of unsuccessful light bulbs before he invented one that worked! But with each unsuccessful attempt, a scientist learns what *doesn't* work. This is an important discovery to move closer to what does.

EXPERIMENT WITH EXPERIMENTS

Some experiments are done in a controlled space such as a **laboratory**. Others are done "in the field." For any experiment, a scientist must determine their **method**—the steps they will take and repeat to ensure the experiment works. Safety measures must be considered as well!

WRITE IT DOWN

Scientists must work carefully and precisely. They **record** all steps, materials, and results of their experiments. This means they can analyze or reproduce the tests later. If they repeat the experiment, changing only what they want to test while keeping all other conditions the same, they might discover patterns in their **data**. They might also come up with new questions to ask!

NEVER STOP QUESTIONING

Science has developed greatly over the years. Even in your lifetime, there has been so much new and changing technology. If scientists continue to question and create, just imagine where they might take us next!

Simple science

A physicist might test forces of gravity and resistance by rolling balls down different slopes.

Question: What slope surface is fastest for rolling a ball down a hill?

Hypothesis: A ball will roll down a smooth surface the fastest.

Materials:
1 round ball
1 tray
3 different materials to line the tray: oil, sandpaper, felt
A stopwatch

Method:

Place the tray on an incline. Rub oil on the tray.
Roll the ball down the oiled tray. Use the stopwatch to time how quickly the ball reaches the bottom.
Repeat 10 times and record the results.
Wipe off the tray and line it with sandpaper. Ensure the tray is on the same incline as before. Repeat the experiment.
Remove the sandpaper and line the tray with felt. Repeat the experiment.

Conclusion:

Every time, the ball reached the end of the hill fastest on the oiled tray. A smooth surface is therefore fastest for a ball going downhill.

Explanation:

The smooth surface was slippery and provided the least resistance to the ball. It rolled quickly down the oiled tray without effort. The sandpaper and felt were much bumpier, causing the ball to slow down.

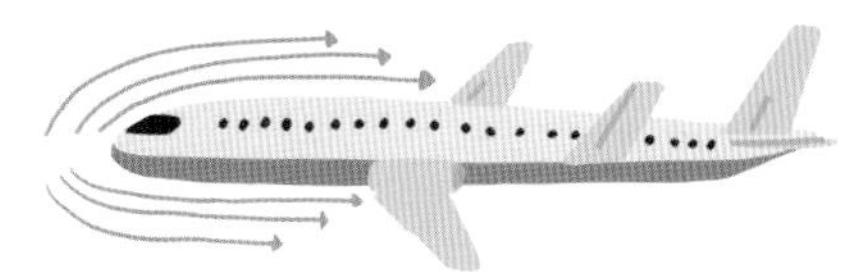

CHAPTER 1

DYNAMICS: FEELING FORCE AND MOTION

Forces are some of the fundamentals of physics. From the pull of gravity to the push of pressure, from floating to sinking, physics is there.

Dynamics is the study of the motion that occurs due to forces—the action that happens thanks to forces in our Universe. In this chapter, we'll look at forces including gravity, pressure, friction, resistance, buoyancy, and magnetism. Then we'll go a step further and learn how these forces work in our world. How does a race car go from stopped to super-fast? How does an elevator go up and down? Get ready for an action-packed ride!

FEEL THE FORCE

Forces allow us to go about life in the way we know it. They help us stay on the ground, walk along that same ground, and drive in cars, ice skate, or even fly, too. Without forces, life would be very different!

WHAT IS A FORCE?

Simply put, a force is a push or pull that can change the speed, direction, or shape of something. Some forces work when objects touch each other, such as bicycle wheels on the pavement. Other forces work when objects aren't touching at all. Have you ever seen a magnet pick up a paperclip from a table, pulling it through the air? That's a force at work!

FINDING BALANCE

Some forces are working all the time. Gravity, for example, is always pulling objects—and you!—toward Earth. Other forces happen with a little more effort. Things get especially exciting when forces become **unbalanced**. Take a look at the game of tug of war. Both teams try to pull the other over the middle line. If the pull forces are the same coming from each side, nobody moves. But if one team pulls harder than the other, we have a winner!

NEWTON'S LAWS OF MOTION

Sir Isaac Newton was a famous physicist born in 1642. He discovered three simple laws that explain how forces can make things move. These are called the **laws of motion**, and they can be used to explain everything from the actions of tiny atoms to super-sized spacecraft.

1. **An object that isn't being pushed or pulled will stay in the same state of motion that it's in.** This means that if an object isn't moving, it will continue to stay still. If it's in motion, it will continue to move at the same speed and in the same direction until a force changes that motion. For example, if you started gliding across a smooth ice rink, you would keep on going until you crashed into something to stop you!

2. **The acceleration or deceleration of an object depends on the force acting on it, and the object's mass.** Acceleration means speeding up, and deceleration means slowing down. Each of these happens quicker with lighter objects (objects with less **mass**). Race cars are much lighter than big heavy trucks, and so they can accelerate much quicker. This law also says that a bigger force will create faster acceleration or deceleration. The harder you push on something, the quicker it moves!

3. **Every action has an equal and opposite reaction.** Forces always work in pairs. If one object pushes on another, the second object pushes back with the same force. Rockets blast off using this principle. The thrust of the explosion within the rocket pushes down on the ground, which pushes back on the rocket with equal force—enough to launch it into space!

GROUNDED BY GRAVITY

Gravity keeps us grounded—literally. Without it, we would float away! Our homes, our pets, falling leaves ... all would float out to space without this special invisible force pulling them down. Space itself would look very different without gravity keeping the Solar System intact.

MASSIVE DISCOVERY

Gravity was explained by Sir Isaac Newton in the late 1600s. It is a force you can find anywhere—the **force** that pulls objects with **mass** or energy toward each other. This force is stronger the closer objects are to each other. On top of that, the greater the mass of an object, the greater the **gravitational pull** it has. For example, Earth is so massive that it pulls all objects toward it, holding you down on the ground. The Earth is also pulled toward you, but only by the tiniest amount.

WORKING AGAINST GRAVITY

Objects speed up as they fall toward the Earth. But you may have noticed that not all objects fall in the same way. A rock seems to drop straight down, while a feather floats and flits back and forth before resting gently on the ground. **Air** works against gravity, pushing back on a moving object. The greater the surface area, the greater the force of air resistance. A parachute can slow down a skydiver due to air resistance. The parachute's curved design also traps air inside it, using air pressure to slow down the skydiver to a safe landing.

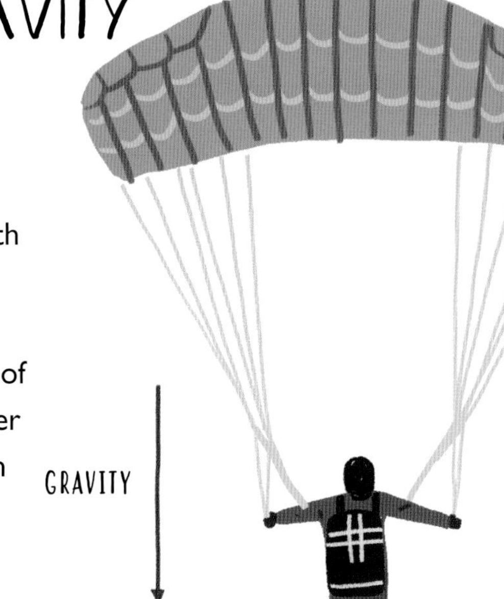

SECURED IN SPACE

Gravity exists everywhere. Not limited to Earth, this powerful force can even be found in space. The Earth exerts gravity on the Moon, keeping it in **orbit** around our planet. The Moon exerts its own force back on Earth, pulling our oceans toward it and affecting the **tides**. Beyond that, the Sun pulls all the planets in the Solar System toward it using its gravity. Gravity holds our Universe together.

OUT OF THIS WORLD!

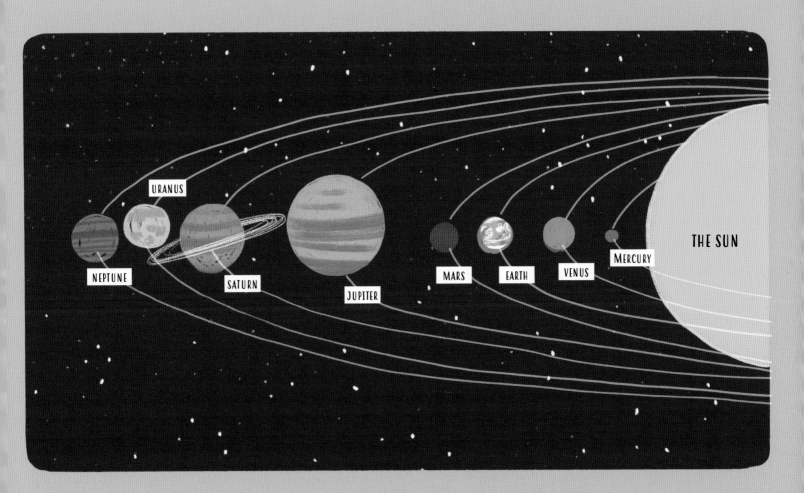

URANUS
NEPTUNE
SATURN
JUPITER
MARS
EARTH
VENUS
MERCURY
THE SUN

OUT OF CURIOSITY

Astronauts grow taller in space! This is because on Earth, the force of gravity pulls the bones in the spine downward and together. In space, low gravity allows these bones to spread out—making the astronaut up to 3% taller.

UNDER PRESSURE

We do not exist in empty space. Even while we stand still on Earth, various forces are at work on us. Gravity pulls us down to the ground, while the ground pushes back up on us. Air presses in from all directions, while our bodies push back on the air. Sometimes we don't notice, and sometimes we feel the pressure!

WHAT IS PRESSURE?

Pressure is the amount of pushing force acting over an area. A force can be strong or weak, spread out or working on a small space. Pressure helps us measure this. If you push strongly on a small area, you create **high** pressure. But if you push lightly with your hands spread out over a bigger area, the pressure will be **weak**. You can use this knowledge to your advantage—if you concentrate your force into a small space, you can suddenly feel much more powerful than if your pressure is spread out!

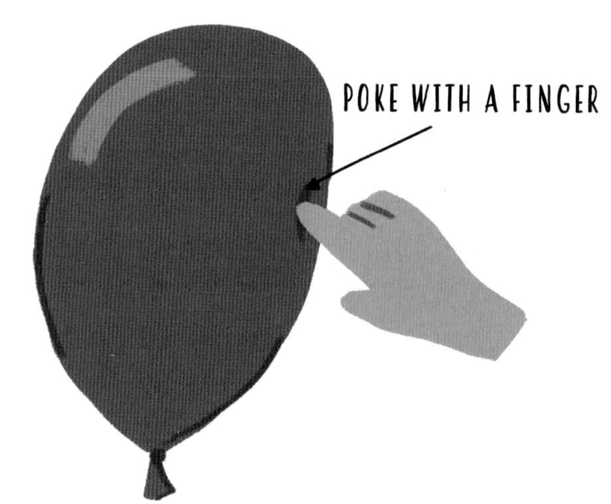

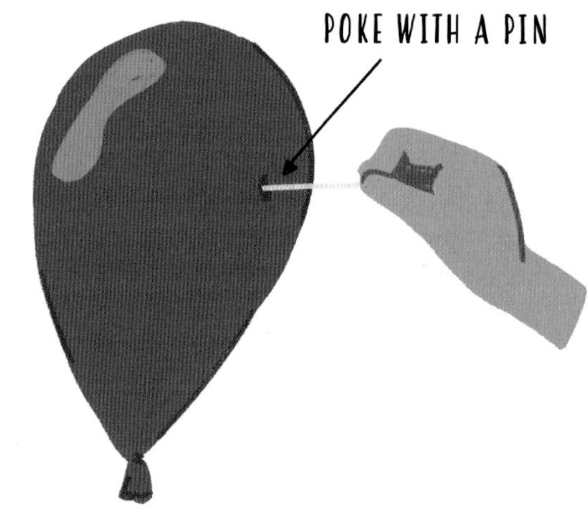

Take a balloon as an example. It is hard to burst a balloon by pushing on it with your finger. This is because the pressure is spread out across your fingertip, and it is not strong enough to pierce the balloon. However, what happens if you poke the balloon with a pin? Suddenly the pressure is much greater, because it is concentrated in one tiny area on the tip of the pin. The pin easily pierces the balloon's rubber, the gas bursts out, and … pop!

WEIGHT ON YOUR SHOULDERS

We might not think of air as having any weight, but in fact gravity makes each air molecule weigh something. In big quantities, air can create pressure. The **atmosphere** is a big blanket of air wrapped around the Earth. It presses down on the surface and creates **air pressure**. Air pressure high up in the atmosphere is weak, since the atmosphere is thin. But closer to the ground, the air is thick, the weight of the air above presses down, and air pressure is high.

The same principle applies to water. **Water pressure** is the force of water's weight pressing down on you. Near the surface, water pressure is weak. But as you venture farther into the deep sea, the water pressure increases. This is because the weight of the water increases, with the water above pressing down. Deep-sea divers wear special suits and air tanks so that they can swim in these high-pressure conditions.

MEASURE THE PRESSURE

Air pressure changes with the weather. Scientists use a **barometer** to measure air pressure and predict the weather. If the air pressure is high, you can expect clear skies and cooler temperatures. But if the air pressure is low, there may be warmer weather and storms! Air molecules tend to move from high pressure to low pressure areas, so if there is a difference in pressure, forecasters would predict windy times ahead.

FIGHTING FRICTION

If you've ever tried running across an ice rink, you'll know how important the force of friction is. Without it, things—and people—would slip and slide all over the place!

WHAT IS FRICTION?

Friction is a force of **resistance** that slows things down. It works in the opposite direction to motion and happens when one object rubs against another.

The resistance depends on how smooth the surfaces are. **Smooth** surfaces create less friction, which means that things can slide over them easily. Ice skates glide across smooth ice, and skis slide easily over slippery snow. However, **rough** surfaces can create a lot of friction. It feels nearly impossible to push a sofa across a carpet, because the sofa is heavy and the carpet is rough!

SMOOTH RIDE

To get around the force of friction, objects can be designed to be as frictionless as possible. Skis slide on snow because they are smooth, light, and flat. This careful design means that there is very little resistance between the skis and the snow, and skiers can rush down hills with ease.

GET A GRIP

On the other hand, some objects are designed to work against friction and provide grip. Your shoes have bumpy treads that help you grip the surface you're walking on, so you don't slip everywhere. A bicycle is full of clever friction hacks for a smooth ride.

The bike chain is **lubricated** with oil. Lubricants are slippery materials that can reduce friction. Oil helps the bicycle chain move smoothly.

The handles, pedals, and seat have textured, bumpy surfaces to stop your hands, feet, and bottom from sliding off.

The bike's wheels are narrow so only a small surface area is in contact with the road. This reduces friction so the bike can keep moving.

WHEELS MOVE ACROSS THE GROUND

FRICTION WITH THE GROUND SLOWS THE WHEELS DOWN

Brake pads grip the wheel when you want to stop. Friction with the brake pads slows the wheels down.

HEATING UP

Friction can also create **heat**. If you rub your hands together, you'll notice them heating up. This is the same as car wheels spinning on the road. The smell of burning rubber comes from wheels spinning so quickly against the road that they overheat.

THE POWER OF RESISTANCE

Some forces, such as gravity, aren't very noticeable as you go about your daily activities. But others make some activities a real challenge! Air and water resistance create a force called **drag**, which can significantly slow you down.

WHAT IS RESISTANCE?

Resistance comes from friction, the force that pushes back on objects in motion and slows them down. The faster the object, the greater the resistance.

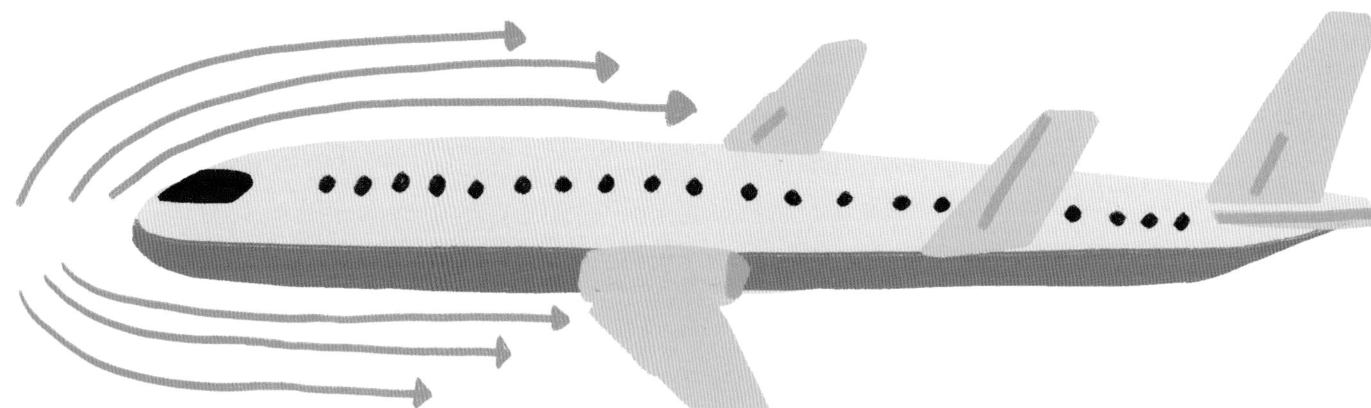

AIR RESISTANCE

Air resistance is a type of friction that occurs between an object and the air. You can experience air resistance working on you as you cycle fast and feel the air on your face. Cars, bicycles, and planes are designed to be **aerodynamic**—with a streamlined shape that reduces drag from the air moving past. The long, rounded shape of a plane means that air that comes into contact with the plane is quickly directed around and away. Thin, pointy objects experience less air resistance than those with wider, flatter surfaces.

OUT OF CURIOSITY

Even though cars are designed to be as streamlined as possible, over half of a car's fuel is used to overcome the force of drag.

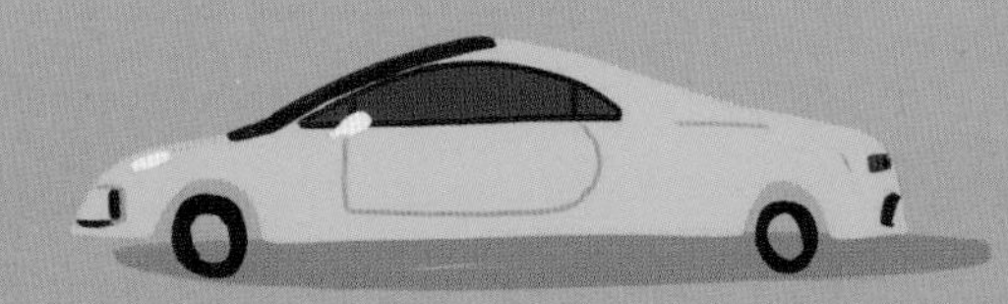

WATER RESISTANCE

Water resistance is a type of friction that occurs between an object and the water. In this case, it's water that slows down a moving object. Just like air resistance, the resistance of water is greater the faster an object is moving and the wider it is. And just like our aerodynamic cars and planes, many sea creatures have streamlined bodies that help them swim swiftly through the sea. The ocean's top predator, the great white shark, has a torpedo-shaped body to power through water and catch its prey!

When you go swimming, there is friction between your skin and the water particles. You need to work hard to overcome the water resistance and pull yourself through the water. You tuck your head in and stretch out your hands and arms, reducing the points where water can push back on you to slow you down. And you're off!

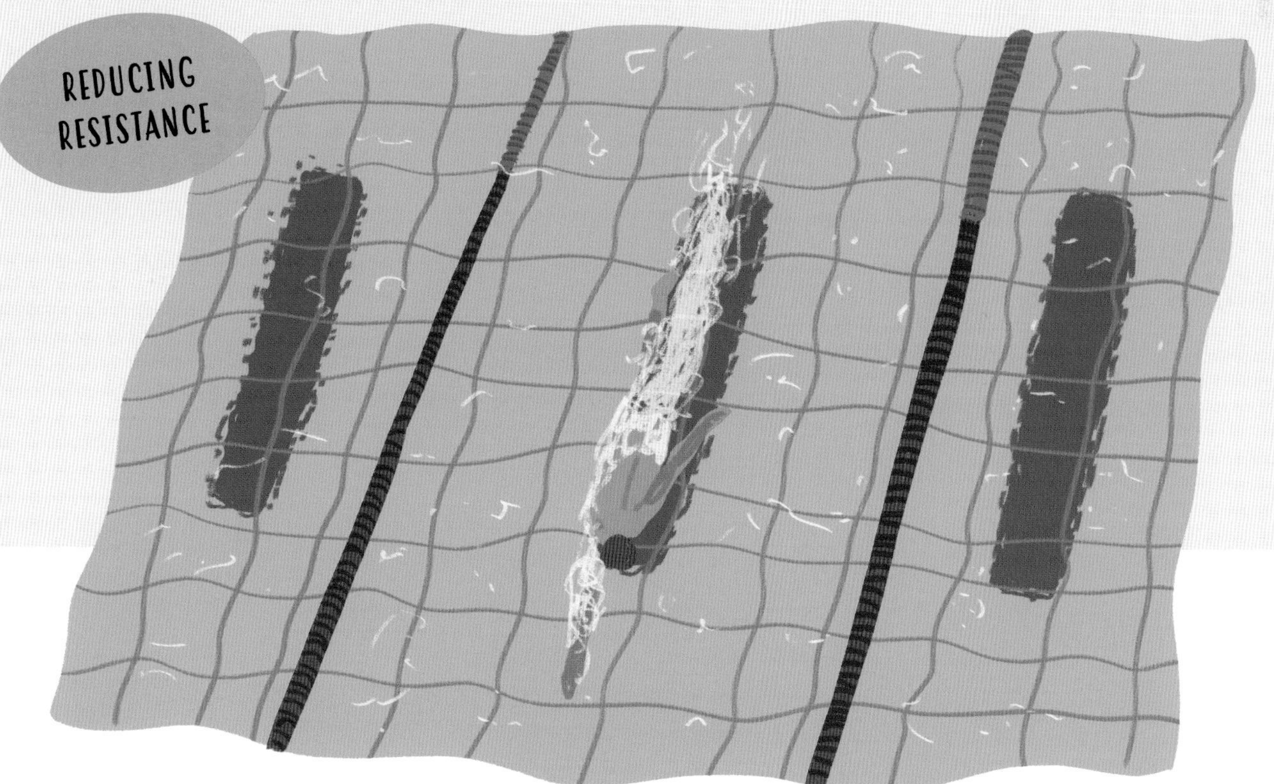

BEING BUOYANT

When an object is in water, there are many different forces working on it. We know that water resistance pushes back on the object when it tries to move. But what about floating and sinking? How do objects sink or stay afloat?

SINK OR SWIM?

WHAT IS BUOYANCY?

Buoyancy is the ability of something to float in water or another liquid. An object that floats is said to be **buoyant**. When you try to swim down to the bottom of the deep end of a pool, you can feel a buoyant force trying to push you back up.

STAYING AFLOAT

Every object in water has two forces acting on it. **Weight**—which is to say, the object's own weight—pulls it down. **Upthrust** is the force of the water pushing up on it. If these forces are equal, the object will be **suspended**. The object will **float**, and rise up to the surface, if the upthrust is greater than the weight. This is why a feather or a light stick can be seen floating above water on a lake.

OUT OF CURIOSITY

Our bodies become buoyant in the Dead Sea. This lake is so full of salt that the water is denser than normal. This makes your weight less than the upthrust, and you float!

BREAKING THE BALANCE

However, if the weight is greater than the upthrust, the object will **sink**. For example, a heavy anchor plunges straight down to the bottom of the lake and can hold a floating boat in place.

KETTLE OF FISH

Fish and other sea creatures have cleverly evolved to suit their underwater world. They need to be able to overcome the competing forces of weight and upthrust to stay in the water without floating or sinking. Normally these forces are about equal on most fish, so they naturally stay between the surface and the sea floor. However, fish have another trick up their sleeves (or fins!). They have a swim bladder that holds oxygen. If the fish begins to sink deeper, the swim bladder absorbs more oxygen. And if the fish begins to float too high, oxygen is released.

OPPOSITES ATTRACT

Magnets are a fascinating phenomenon, both in nature and when created by humans. They can cause objects to come together, push apart, or even dance in the sky. Magnets are a mystery of the world that scientists have come to understand through physics.

MAGNETIC FORCE

Magnetism is a force between two metallic objects. It is created by electric charge and can cause objects to **attract** (pull together) or **repel** (push apart). Each magnet has two **poles**: north and south. When two like poles are close together (such as north and north or south and south), the magnets repel. When two opposite poles are close together (north and south or south and north), the magnets attract.

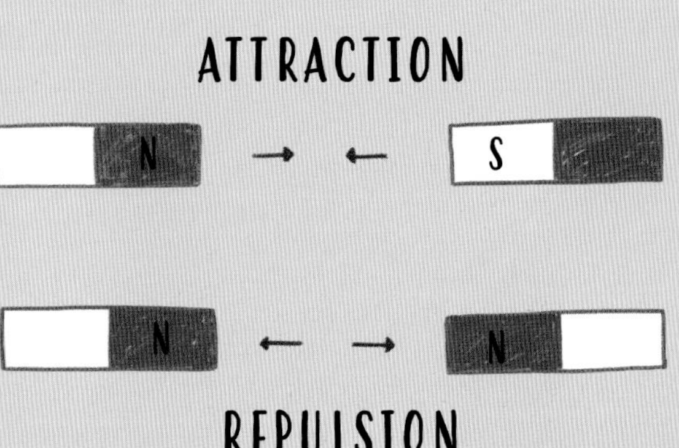

MAGNETIC MATERIALS

Not all materials are magnetic. In fact, only a select few are! First, to be magnetic they must be made of **metal**. And second, the metal must be able to hold a magnetic charge. Iron, steel, nickel, and cobalt are magnetic metals. Metals such as silver and gold have no magnetic force.

Some metals are always magnetic—these are called **hard, permanent** magnets. The magnets on your fridge are a good example of this! Other metals become magnetic when a magnet is near them, but don't have magnetism on their own. These are **soft and temporary** magnetic materials.

OUR MAGNETIC WORLD

Magnets play an important part in our world. In fact, some can even help care for the planet, such as in a recycling plant. By using a huge magnetic crane, we can separate and pull out magnetic metals—ready for recycling. This saves them from going to a landfill. Magnets are also used for sophisticated, speedy trains—the futuristic maglev train uses magnetism to repel and levitate (hover) above its tracks.

Beyond that, Earth itself is a giant magnet! This is because of the movement of molten iron in the planet's core. This creates a **magnetic field** of invisible force between Earth's two poles. This field can attract magnetically charged particles from the Sun, which burn up as they enter the atmosphere. The resulting light show is called the aurora borealis, or the Northern Lights.

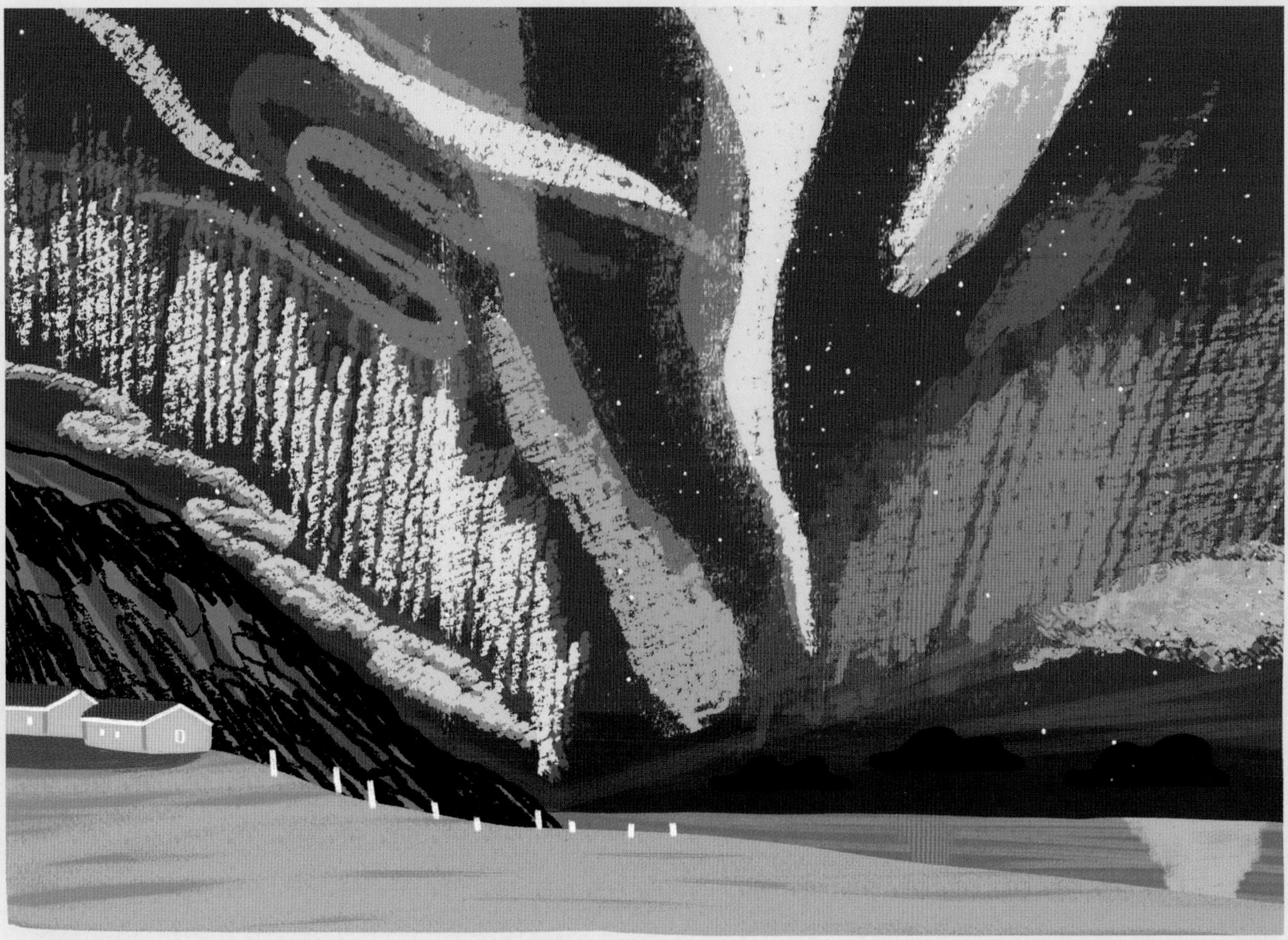

OUT OF CURIOSITY

If you stand at Earth's North Pole, the north end of a compass wants to point downward (instead of forward). And if you stand at the South Pole, the south end points down!

FORCES IN ACTION

If we work with forces, rather than against them, we can make everyday jobs easier. Machines have been built to harness forces, reducing the amount of effort and force needed, in order to move things more easily than if you tried to do the tasks by hand. Physics has helped build and run our world.

HELPING HAND

Simple machines help by **magnifying** the force they put in. You put in one force, and the machine helps make it bigger. This helps lift or pull heavy or resistant objects.

LEVER UP

One way to help lift heavy objects is by using a **lever**. A lever is a bar that sits on a fixed point, called a **fulcrum.** If you push on one end of the bar, the other side lifts up. Because the objects are at a distance, and they use the pivot point of the fulcrum, less force is needed to lift a load sitting on one end of the lever than if you tried to lift it on its own. Levers can be used in simple gadgets such as pliers—when you press the handles together, your weak force is magnified by the fulcrum to a powerful gripping force on the other end.

GEARING UP

Gears are wheels with teeth. They connect to other gears or chains by interlinking their teeth. When one gear turns, it makes the gear connected to it turn in the opposite direction. Smaller gears with more teeth turn more quickly but with less force. Larger gears with fewer teeth turn more slowly but with more force. Cars, bicycles, analog clocks, and many more day-to-day objects make use of gears to make them go. As the gears turn, they magnify the force put in to make things go. For example, your push on a bicycle pedal turns one gear, which then makes the rear wheel turn, which is connected by a chain. The bicycle moves forward!

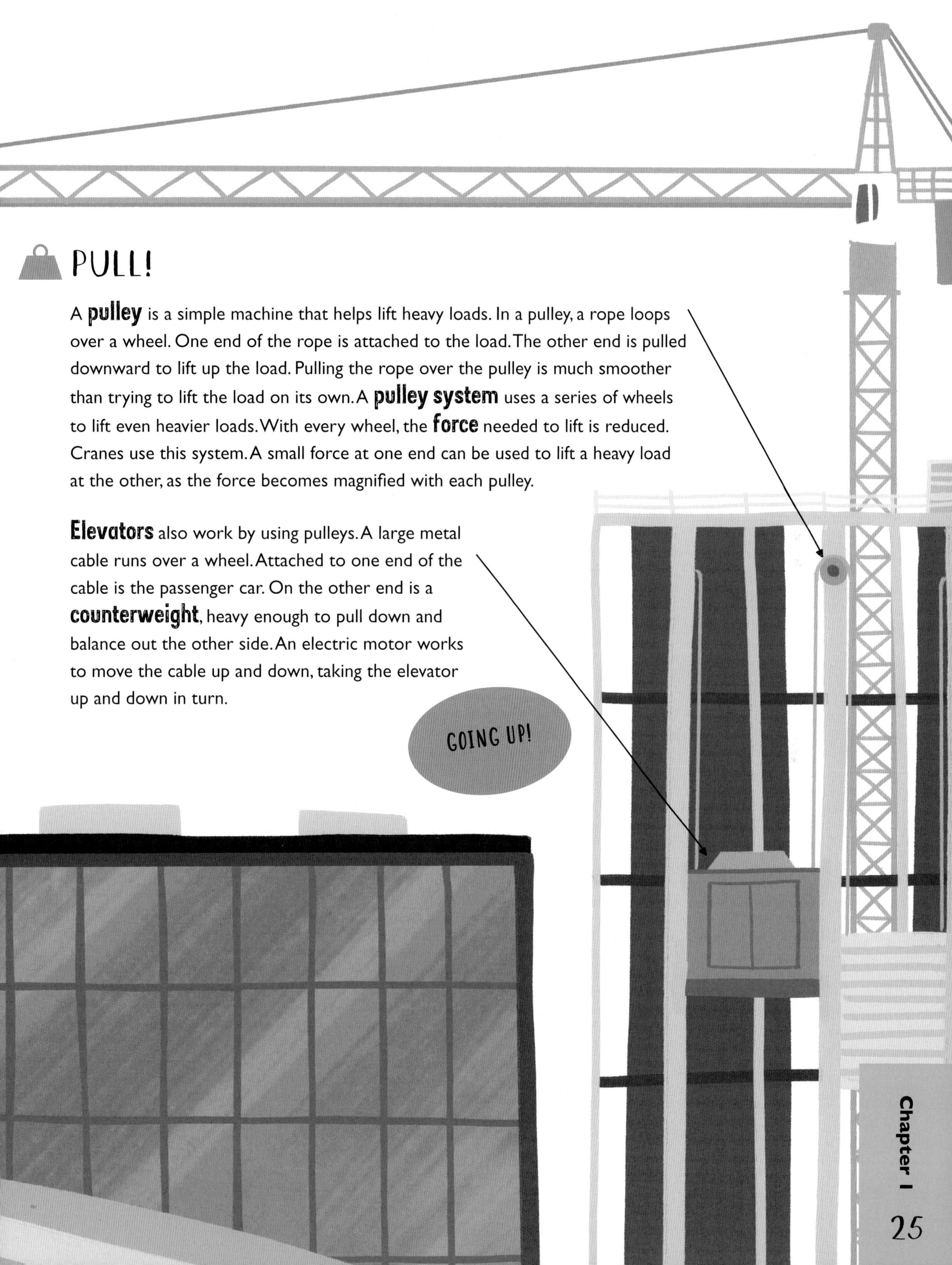

PULL!

A **pulley** is a simple machine that helps lift heavy loads. In a pulley, a rope loops over a wheel. One end of the rope is attached to the load. The other end is pulled downward to lift up the load. Pulling the rope over the pulley is much smoother than trying to lift the load on its own. A **pulley system** uses a series of wheels to lift even heavier loads. With every wheel, the **force** needed to lift is reduced. Cranes use this system. A small force at one end can be used to lift a heavy load at the other, as the force becomes magnified with each pulley.

Elevators also work by using pulleys. A large metal cable runs over a wheel. Attached to one end of the cable is the passenger car. On the other end is a **counterweight**, heavy enough to pull down and balance out the other side. An electric motor works to move the cable up and down, taking the elevator up and down in turn.

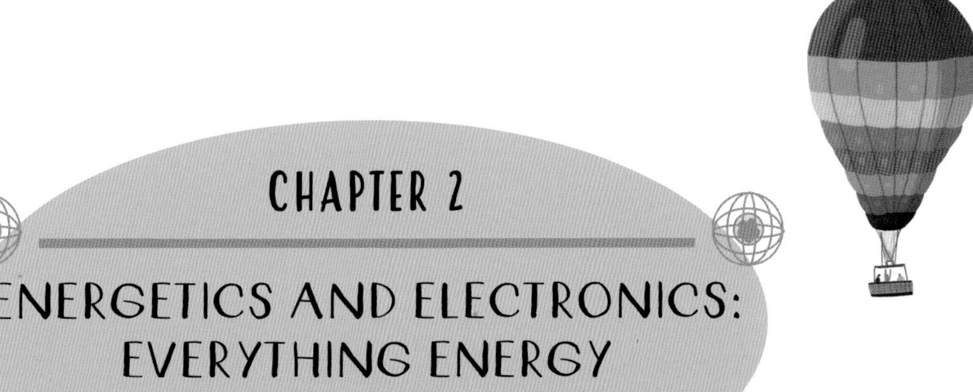

CHAPTER 2

ENERGETICS AND ELECTRONICS: EVERYTHING ENERGY AND ELECTRICITY

Energy lights up our world. Not only that—it makes things happen! Everything that moves uses energy, from plants growing to people dancing to cars racing. Energy can be used or changed, transferred or stored. Energy includes heat, light, electricity, and more. Energy really is everywhere!

Energetics is the study of energy—how it behaves, transfers, and changes. In this chapter, we'll look at where energy comes from, how it can be used, types of energy, and how we power our world. We'll also take a look at **electronics**, and how energy can travel through circuits. Be prepared to be **energized** as you make your way through these pages.

ALL ABOUT ATOMS

Energy often involves the movement of the particles that make up matter. Everything in our Universe is made of **atoms**. The rain, your house, your nose, the stars ... Atoms make up the matter that makes up our world.

WHAT'S THE MATTER?

Matter is what things are made of. All matter consists of tiny particles called **atoms**. Atoms are SUPER teeny-tiny. Inside just one small grain of sand there are 60 million trillion atoms (60,000,000,000,000,000,000)! Depending on how atoms are arranged, matter can take on different forms—solid, liquid, or gas; see-through or not.

INSIDE AN ATOM

Although atoms are small, they have even smaller things inside them! These are called subatomic particles.

Electrons whiz around the nucleus in shell-like orbits. They are particles with a **negative** charge. Positive and negative charges attract, so electrons are pulled toward the protons. Electrons are even smaller than protons and neutrons.

The **nucleus** is the central part of the atom. It is made up of protons and neutrons.

Protons are one type of particle that make up the nucleus. They have a **positive** electrical charge.

Neutrons are the other type of particle that make up the nucleus. They have no electrical charge. Neutrons have about the same mass as protons.

PUTTING IT TOGETHER

The number of protons in an atom's nucleus determines what type of substance that atom is. An atom with 79 protons inside, for example, is gold. Oxygen has only eight protons in its nucleus. These substances, such as gold and oxygen, are called **elements**.

Atoms often join with other atoms to create **molecules**. A molecule has two or more atoms bonded together. The combination of atoms in a molecule determines what type of substance the molecule is. When one oxygen atom joins with two hydrogen atoms, it forms a molecule of liquid water. A drop of water contains millions of these molecules. However, when two oxygen atoms join to one carbon atom, you haven't got liquid at all—you've got the gas carbon dioxide. And when you have two oxygen atoms joined together, you have our all-important O_2—the gas we need to breathe.

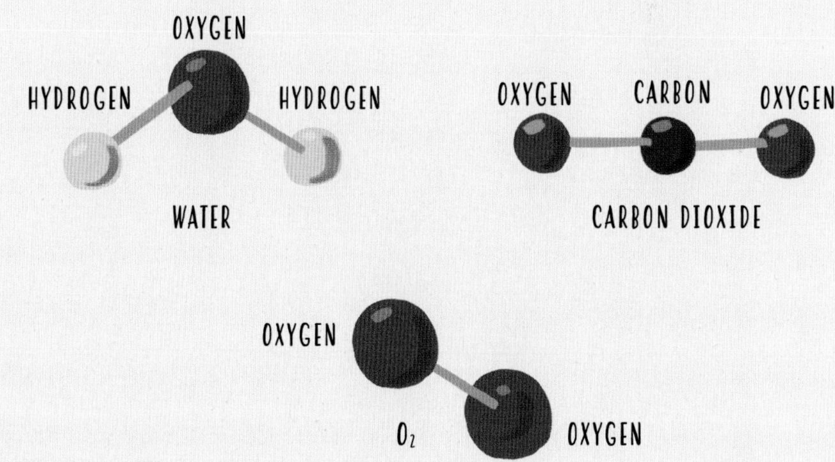

OUT OF CURIOSITY

All the atoms in your body have been recycled over billions and billions of years.

ENERGIZING OUR WORLD

Energy powers people, plants, cars, homes, and so much more. Without it, our world would be cold, dark ... and lifeless.

WHAT IS ENERGY?

Energy makes things happen. It helps anything in the Universe perform an action, from moving to glowing to heating up. It comes in many forms.

Heat energy makes things warm up. Energy from something hot moves to something cold. For example, as a fire burns, heat and light are released and transferred to people sitting nearby.

Light energy comes from glowing objects. It moves in a straight line and bounces off objects into our eyes.

Sound energy is produced by vibrations, which travel through the air to our ears.

Electrical energy comes from charged particles building up and moving together. The current of charge flows through wires to bring power to objects. It can also cause lightning!

POWERING THE PLANET

The **Sun** provides a huge amount of energy to our planet. It transfers both light and heat, which help us see and stay warm.

The Sun is made of mainly hydrogen atoms. It is so hot that these atoms lose their electrons, leaving only the nucleus of protons. These nuclei join together and make helium atoms. As the atoms fuse and create a heavier nucleus, energy is released. This process is called **nuclear fusion**, and it releases a whole lot of energy!

HOW DOES IT WORK?

Scientists believe that all energy in our Universe began with the Big Bang, 13.8 billion years ago. Energy today is not created or destroyed. Instead, it can be transferred from one object to another. For example, energy from the Sun is transferred to plants, which use it as food to help them grow. Animals might then eat the plants, and the energy is transferred to them. Energy can also be stored for later use, such as in a battery.

$E=mc^2$

Albert Einstein, born in 1879, is one of the most well-known scientists of the 20th century. His equation, $E=mc^2$, might be even more famous than he is! Einstein showed that matter and energy are the same thing. Matter is made up of particles that are essentially just energy, such as protons and electrons. His formula shows that the energy (E) emitted by matter can be determined by the amount of matter in kilograms (m) multiplied by the speed of light squared (c^2)—a very huge number! In simpler terms, this means that a small amount of matter can release a huge amount of energy, such as huge blasts created by an atomic bomb.

LYING IN STORE 

You can think of energy a little bit like money. You can save your money, keeping it safe to spend later. Or you can spend it right away and make something happen. Energy works in a similar way. It can be saved with the potential to be used later, or it can be used. Let's have a look at some more types of energy.

IT'S GOT POTENTIAL

Potential energy is **stored** energy. It builds up and then waits to be used. Picture a roller coaster. As the cart rides up the first hill, potential energy builds up. Stored energy is at its maximum when the cart sits at the top. Then, the energy is released and the cart plunges down the hill. Hold on to your stomach!

ELASTIC POTENTIAL ENERGY

When you push down on a spring, or pull on elastic, you have **elastic potential energy**. It is stored in a material that is squashed or stretched. The more the material is stretched or squashed, the more stored energy it has. Once the material has been pushed or pulled, energy is stored, ready to take the object back to its original position as soon as you let go.

GRAVITATIONAL POTENTIAL ENERGY

All objects have **gravitational potential energy**, as the force of gravity pulls them toward Earth. The higher (and heavier) the object, the more gravitational potential energy it has. When you lift a ball above your head, you give it gravitational potential energy. As soon as you let go, this energy is released, and the ball falls to the ground (or on your head!).

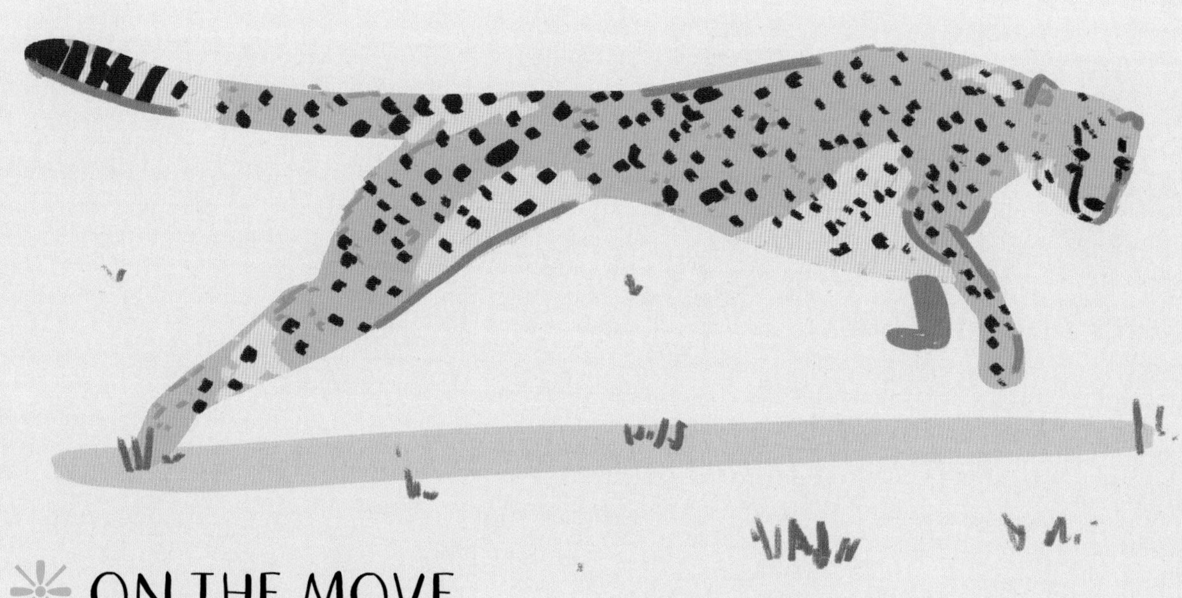

ON THE MOVE

Potential energy is often converted into **kinetic energy.** This is the energy of a moving object. The faster the object is moving, the more kinetic energy it has. When the car at the top of the roller coaster begins to roll down the hill, the potential energy turns into kinetic energy. Combined with gravity, this energy makes the car speed up. Anything in the Universe that moves has kinetic energy. A cheetah changes potential energy stored in its muscles into kinetic energy when it runs, speeding across the ground.

BREAKING BONDS

Chemical energy is stored in all substances, in the bonds that hold atoms together in their molecules. When there is a chemical reaction and the bonds are broken, the energy is released. Fuel and food have plenty of chemical energy. When we eat, our bodies break down the bonds in chemicals in the food, and energy is released and transferred to us.

FINITE POWER

We know that energy powers our world. But how do we harness it? There are many different resources for energy, including sources that will eventually run out and others that keep on giving. Let's first focus on the energy that we can't renew.

RUNNING LOW

Non-renewable energy comes from resources that can't be replenished when they run out. They form too slowly for us to continue using them at our current rate. This includes substances such as oil, coal, and natural gas, which are used to power cars, planes, factories, and more.

FOSSIL FUELS

YEARS IN THE MAKING

Fossil fuels are natural fuels such as coal and oil. They were formed from the remains of organisms that lived millions of years ago. Over time, the organisms were buried under layers and layers of soil and rock. People dig down, or mine, to extract the substances and fuel.

Fossil fuels contain a whole lot of **stored energy**. Coal, for example, was once plants. These plants stored energy from the Sun in the form of chemical energy, which was held when they were buried underground. Oil and natural gas come from ocean plants and animals that were buried beneath the ocean floor. Their stored energy was buried with them.

POWER UP

When fossil fuels are burned, chemical energy is converted into kinetic energy by harnessing the heat. Power stations burn fossil fuels to harness heat into power.

TOO MUCH HEAT

Burning fossil fuels produces a lot of the gas **carbon dioxide**. Carbon dioxide traps the Sun's heat energy in our atmosphere. The more carbon dioxide is pumped into the atmosphere, with factories and cars burning coal and oil, the more our planet heats up. This is called the **greenhouse effect**. This effect is leading to **global warming**, with the planet's overall temperature rising. With global warming comes **climate change**, and devastating effects. As the planet heats up, the climate is disrupted, and entire ecosystems are affected.

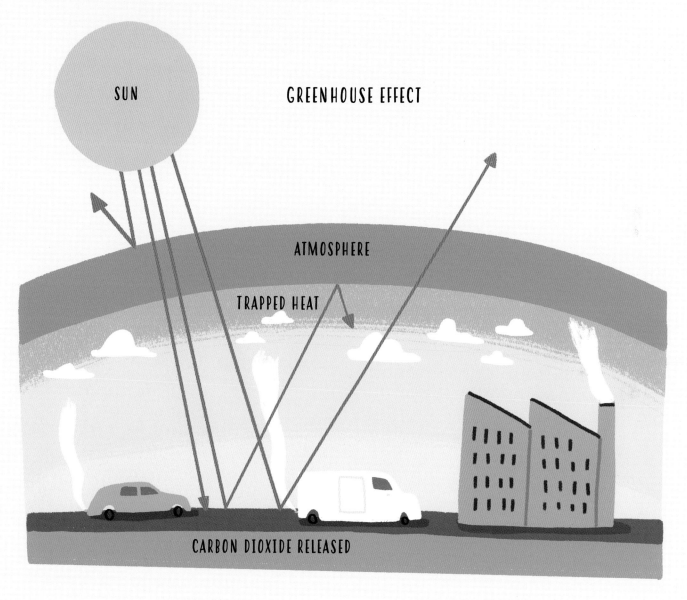

GOING NUCLEAR

Nuclear power is different from fossil fuels. It is created by nuclear reactions. In these nuclear reactions, **nuclear fuels**, such as uranium and plutonium, release energy. This energy is turned into electrical power in power stations. These reactions do not release carbon dioxide, but they can still be dangerous. Their waste is radioactive and must be stored safely.

THE NEVER-ENDING STORY

Scientists work hard to find new, safer, and friendlier ways to power the planet. There are many resources in our world that can be harnessed—without running out.

UP FOR RENEWAL

Renewable energy comes from resources that won't run out, or can be replenished. This includes the Sun, wind, and more. Energy that can be produced without damaging the future of the planet is called **sustainable energy**.

WIND POWER

The wind is movements of air. Its kinetic energy is used to turn the blades on **wind turbines**. The kinetic energy is transferred to the blades, and then to a generator, which converts the kinetic energy into electricity. This type of energy produces no harmful gases, but it does rely on the wind. If there is no wind, there is no electricity!

BIOMASS

Biomass is plant or animal matter burned to produce heat and electricity. This can include wood, which can be replaced by planting new trees. It also includes poop! Sewage can be turned into pellets, which are burned to produce heat. The heat produces steam, which turns turbines and powers electrical generators. Biomass is not only renewable, but it is also helping the planet by **recycling** waste.

WATER POWER

Water's kinetic energy can be used in a variety of ways. **Wave machines** make use of the up and down motion from waves to drive power to generators. **Tide barrages** take advantage of the water's tides. They are built in river mouths to capture the kinetic energy of the tide going in and out. As water rushes through tubes in the barrage, it powers electrical generators. **Dams** are built to harness the gravitational potential power of large amounts of water. The water is trapped high up, and when it is released, it flows over turbines, which turn the movement into electricity.

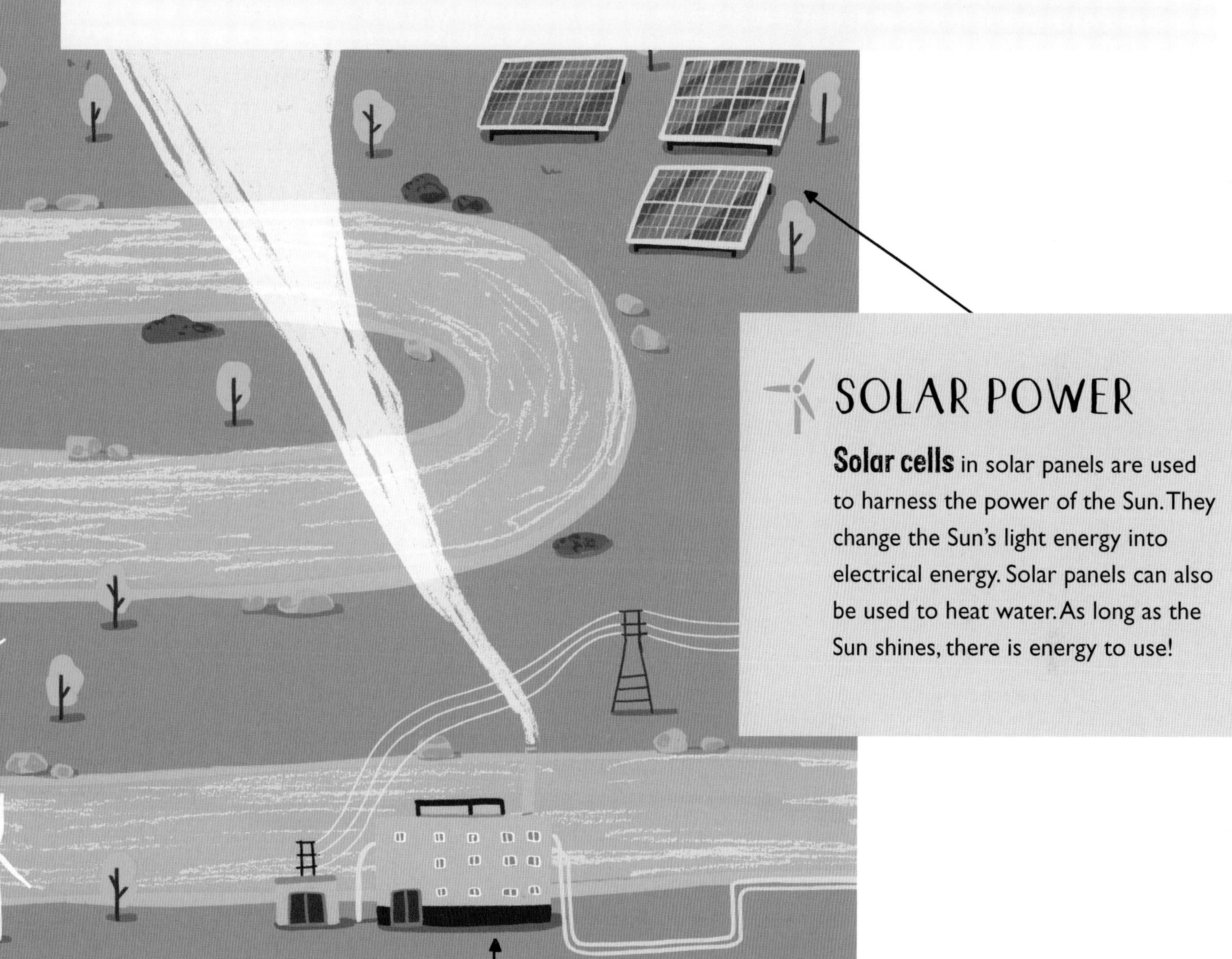

SOLAR POWER

Solar cells in solar panels are used to harness the power of the Sun. They change the Sun's light energy into electrical energy. Solar panels can also be used to heat water. As long as the Sun shines, there is energy to use!

GEOTHERMAL POWER

Geothermal energy makes use of heat from inside the Earth. A generating station pumps cold water below the Earth's surface through pipes. Heat energy underground transfers to the cold water, turning it to steam. The steam then rises up and spins a turbine. This renewable resource works only in areas of the Earth where hot enough rocks below ground are close to the surface.

FEEL THE HEAT

Heat is a type of energy we come across—and feel—in our daily lives. We might use a fire to heat up, or enjoy the warmth of the sunshine on our skin. At other times, we might want to cool down!

WHAT IS HEAT?

Heat energy comes from the movement of atoms and molecules. The faster they move, the hotter the substance is. Cold objects contain molecules that are moving slowly and have very little heat energy. If the molecules could slow down completely, and come to a stop, they would reach a temperature called absolute zero.

HOT TO COLD

Heat energy always tries to move from something hot to something cold. It does this in three ways.

Conduction: Conduction requires the movement of **electrons** between atoms. **Metals** are good conductors. Heat travels directly through them, spreading out from hot to cold. If your hand is colder than a hot pot, the heat travels from the pot to you when you touch it. Ouch!

Convection: Convection involves the movement of **atoms** or **molecules**. It happens in **liquids** and **gases**. As a liquid or gas heats up, the hot gas or liquid rises while cold gas or liquid sinks down to take its place. As water boils in the pot, steam and hot water rise to the top, and cold water takes their place below.

RISING UP

Soaring in the skies above, with only a basket, a burner, and an envelope full of air, a **hot air balloon** rises thanks to heat energy. Fire from a gas burner heats up the air inside the balloon. The hot air is trapped within the curved fabric. As the air heats up, the molecules move faster and spread out, filling the balloon. Due to **convection,** the hot air rises, pushing the balloon upward. The hot air inside the balloon is less dense than the cold air outside the balloon, so it continues to rise in the sky. As the balloon floats along, the air begins to cool, and the balloon dips down. A pilot gives a brief burst of flame from the burner to warm up the air again, and the balloon rises once more.

OUT OF CURIOSITY

In 1783, the hot air balloon was the first technology that successfully allowed people to fly! The very first balloon flight, just months before, carried a chicken, a sheep, and a duck into the sky.

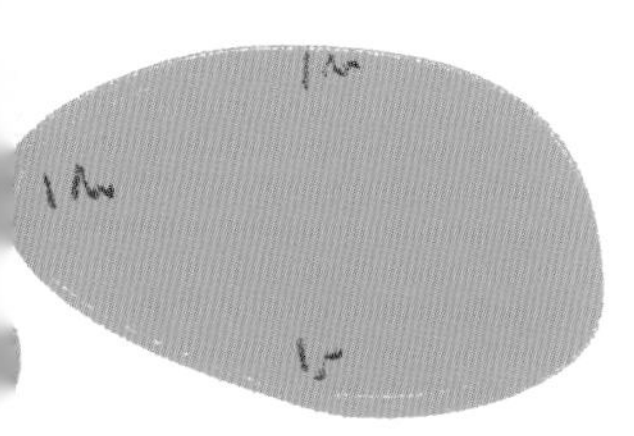

Radiation: Radiation is the movement of energy as **waves**. It doesn't require any particles at all. Heat travels through air and space by invisible rays. Hot objects give off this **infrared radiation**, and this is how we feel heat. The rays from the sun or the heat from a fire **radiate** outward and warm us up.

IT'S ELECTRIC

Hundreds of years ago, instead of flicking a switch to turn on a light, people lit candles. Instead of turning on the heat, they built fire. The discovery of how to harness electricity changed our world.

WHAT IS ELECTRICITY?

Electricity is a type of energy. It can flow from place to place, or build up in one area. It is created by the tiny electrons that carry a negative electric charge. As these electrons whiz around atoms, they can jump from one atom to another. When trillions of electrons move in the same direction, they create an **electric current**.

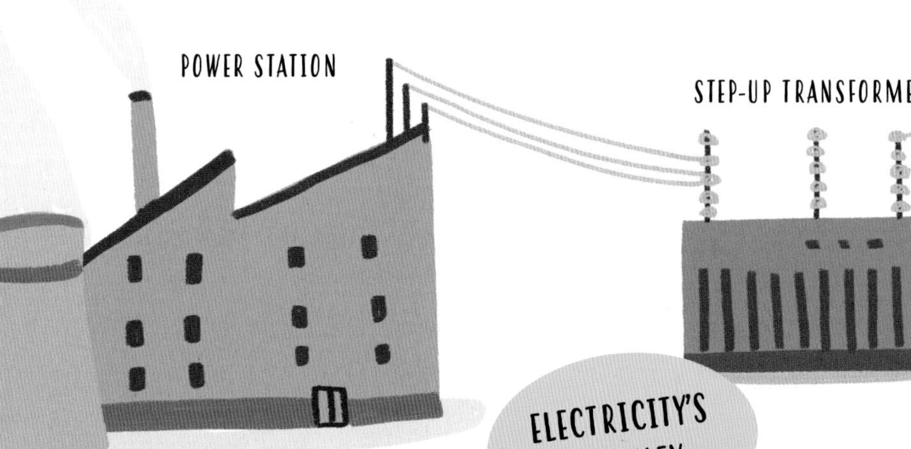

COME ON IN

Electricity exists in nature, but it's when it's harnessed and converted into power that it really becomes useful for us. **Generators** at power stations can capture energy from fossil fuels, sunlight, wind, and water and turn it into electrical energy.

Electricity travels from **power stations** to our homes through **cables**. Cables can run overground, held up by **pylons**, and underground, into buildings. These power lines take electricity all the way to the plug sockets where you plug in lamps, phone chargers, televisions, and more.

Step-up transformers along the way increase the voltage. With a higher voltage, there is lower current, and less energy is wasted as heat.

Step-down transformers reduce the voltage so it can enter your house safely.

ELECTRIC CURRENT

Electric current travels from place to place. It is the type of electricity that comes out of sockets. It can also come from **batteries**. Batteries use chemicals to produce electricity. The energy from the battery becomes the flow of electric current.

STATIC ELECTRICITY

The other kind of electricity is static electricity. This is when electricity builds up in one place. When two objects of certain materials rub together, the charged particles can move from one to the other. One object gains electrons and becomes negatively charged, leaving the other object positively charged.

When you rub a balloon on your head, the electrons from your hair move to the balloon. The balloon becomes negatively charged, and your hair becomes positively charged. When you lift the balloon higher above your head, your hair follows and sticks to it—its positive charge is attracted to the balloon's negative charge!

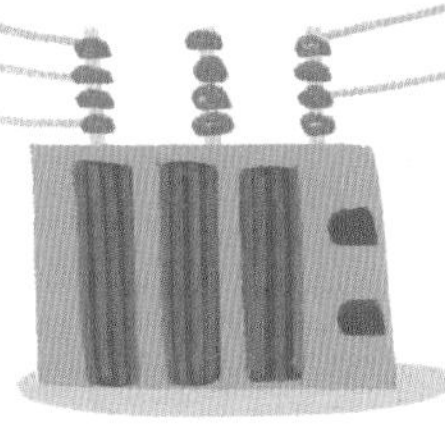

FLASH!

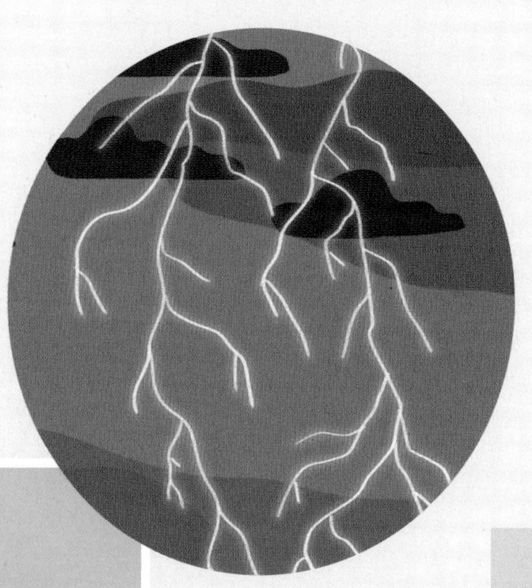

Lightning comes from static electricity. Ice particles in a cloud rub together and build up an electric charge. When this charge becomes too big, it jumps out to other clouds or to Earth as a flash of lightning.

OUT OF CURIOSITY

Lightning is so powerful that it produces heat, light, and sound. It comes with a crash of thunder, and it can be five times hotter than the surface of the Sun!

CIRCUITS OF POWER

Electricity is a lot like water. It flows along paths and likes to take the simplest route. And just as water flows through pipes, electricity flows through cables and wires.

WHAT IS A CIRCUIT?

A **circuit** is a loop that electricity flows through. If the loop is complete, the electricity can move. If the loop is broken, the electricity stops. The stream of electricity moves around as a **current**.

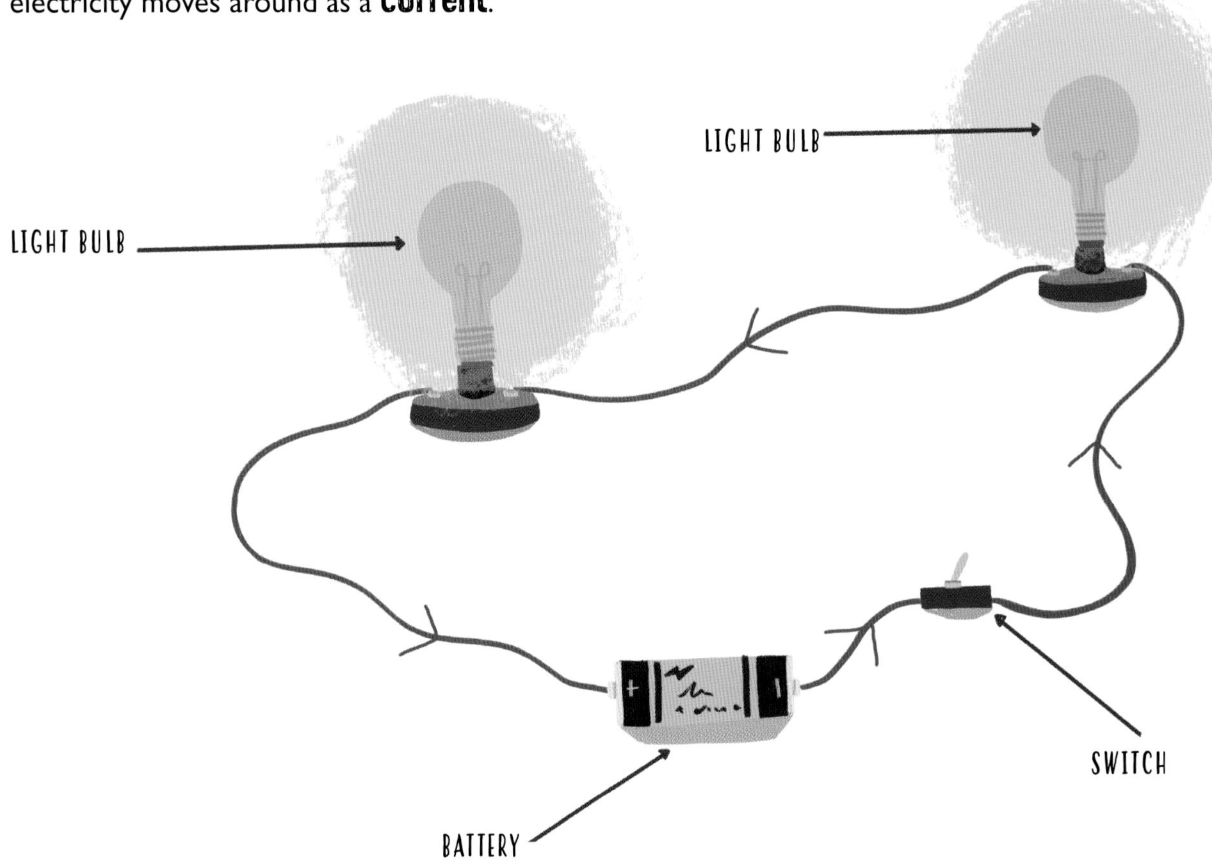

Every circuit needs a **power source**, such as a battery, with positive and negative ends. **Wires** connect the power source to the electrical components you'd like to power, such as a light bulb, and back again to complete the circuit. Electricity is carried along the wires by electrons and flows from negative to positive.

A **switch** turns the circuit on or off. When the switch is open, it creates a gap in the circuit, and the electricity stops. When the switch is closed, the circuit is complete and electricity can flow.

Light bulbs in the circuit above light up when the current of electricity reaches them. They change the electric energy into heat and light.

WILL IT FLOW?

Electricity passes through some materials much easier than others. **Conductors** are materials that allow electricity to pass through them easily, such as metal. Many wires are made of the metal copper. **Insulators** do not allow electricity to pass through them easily, such as plastic or fabric. Wires are coated in plastic so that the electricity is trapped inside—and doesn't reach you directly!

SERIES CIRCUIT

A simple circuit with just one loop is called a **series circuit**. In this type of circuit, everything is connected to the same path. If you add an extra light bulb in a series circuit, the lights will dim, as the energy flowing through is shared between them. And if you add an extra power source, such as another battery, more power is produced to brighten the lights!

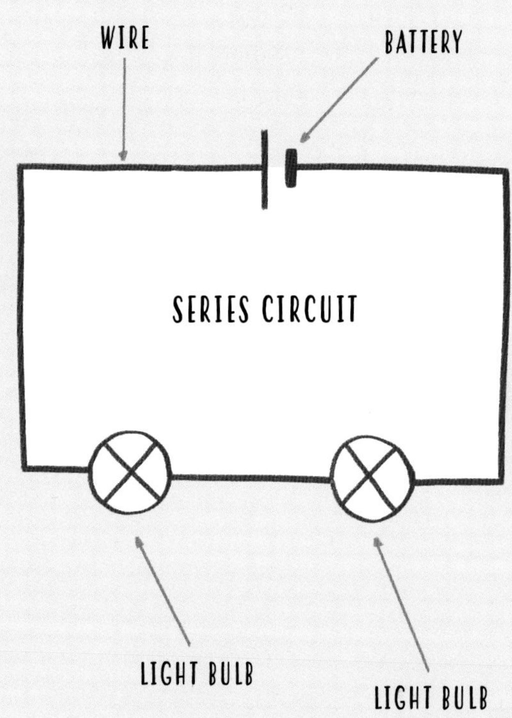

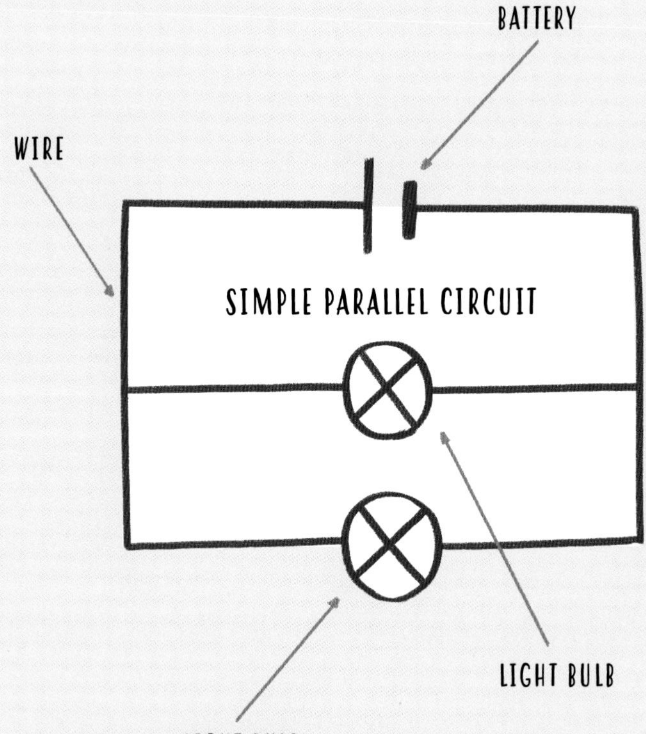

PARALLEL CIRCUIT

In a **parallel circuit**, energy flows along different paths, in **parallel**. Different components are connected on different wires. In this type of circuit, each light bulb receives the full power from the battery source. If one path is broken, energy will continue to flow along the other, so only the light on the broken path will go out. A battery power source will only last half as long as in a series circuit because it is putting out twice as much power to keep two lights glowing brightly.

ENERGY AT HOME

Energy is all around you. Just in your home, you can see energy working in many different ways to power your life. Can you imagine life without it?

When you listen to **music**, your phone or sound system is powered by electrical energy, either through a cable or a battery. Sound energy comes from the speaker and reaches your ears through vibrations in the air.

Lights and **appliances** use electrical energy. They are part of circuits. When a switch is on, electricity flows through and makes them glow or go.

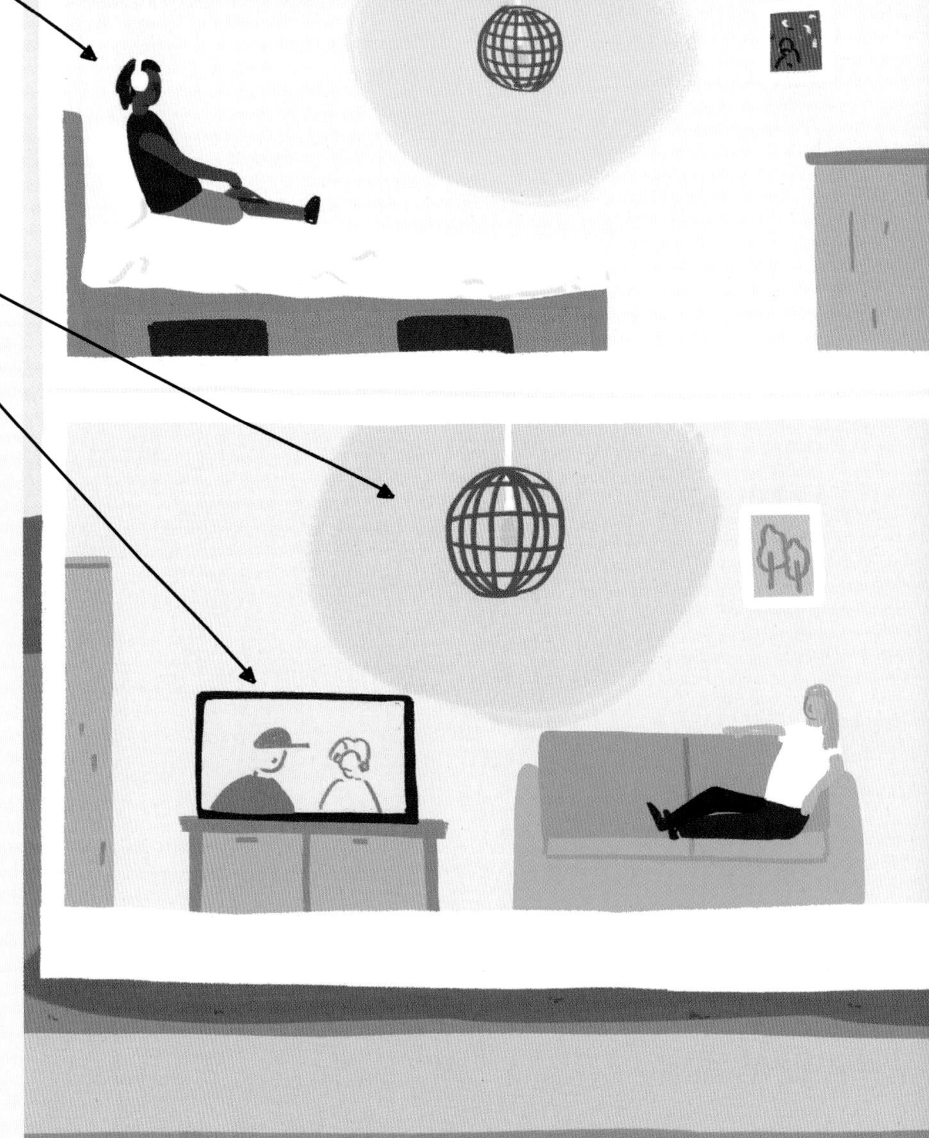

SAVING ENERGY

Energy costs money, and it can cause air pollution and global warming when fossil fuels are burned at generating stations. It is important to save as much energy as possible. This means turning off appliances, lights, and hot water when you are not using them. You can also try to use planet-friendly sources of power whenever you can, such as solar power, and walking or cycling rather than going in a car.

Solar power works in many ways in a house. You can use a solar-powered phone charger to convert energy from the Sun into power for your phone. The Sun also works to heat up rooms and transfer its energy to plants.

Many objects use **batteries**. An electric toothbrush is powered by the chemical energy stored in the battery inside.

Cooking uses electrical and heat energy. An electric oven plugs into the wall, using electrical energy for power. Heat energy is then released and transferred to food to cook it. Gas ovens burn gas to release energy to cook in the same way.

When you or a pet eats **food,** the chemical energy stored inside the food is then stored as chemical energy inside the body. It turns to kinetic and heat energy to help you move and grow.

Riding a **scooter** turns the stored energy in your muscles into kinetic energy to make your body move. Your force pushes the scooter forward!

CHAPTER 3

OPTICS: LOOKING AT LIGHT

Think of the Sun shining; The light that helps you read this page; Fireflies flickering at night. Light is incredibly important and useful in our lives. But how does it work? What is it exactly?

Optics is the study of light and sight—what light is made of, how it behaves, and how we can see. In this chapter we'll shed a light on the electromagnetic spectrum, waves, the speed of light (hint: it's the fastest thing in the Universe!), sources of light, shades, shadows, and rainbows, and then journey into how light helps us to see our world.

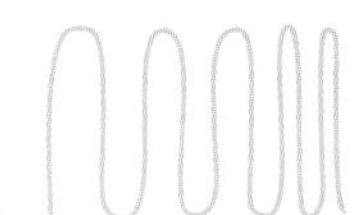

WAVES OF ENERGY

Before we can understand how light works, we need to know how it fits into the greater spectrum of our world.

ALONG THE SPECTRUM

The **electromagnetic spectrum** is a range of types of radiation. **Electromagnetic radiation** is tiny packets of energy, called photons, that travel in a wave-like pattern. Light and sound are good examples of this.

All waves have a **wavelength**—the distance from one peak to the next. When energy travels in waves, the wavelength can vary. The shorter the wavelength, the more energy it has. As you go along the electromagnetic spectrum, the wavelength decreases from long to short, and the energy increases.

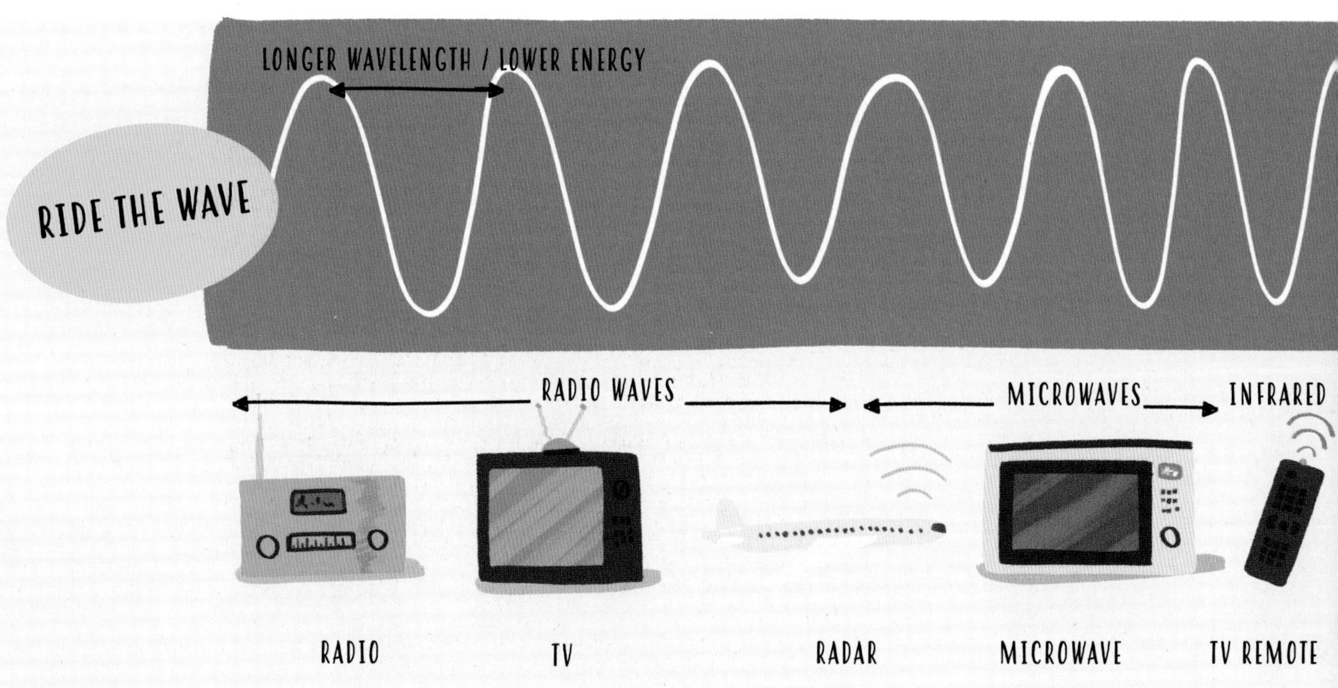

Radio waves: Radio waves have the longest wavelength—around 0.6 mi (1 km). They are emitted from stars and gas in space. You also know them as radio waves, literally! They travel long distances and bring sound to the radios in our homes and cars, as well as pictures to TV. They allow us to communicate.

Microwaves: Microwaves have a shorter wavelength than radio waves. They are also used for communication, such as by communication satellites and telephones. You'll also recognize them as the waves used in your microwave oven, although microwave ovens use a shorter wavelength than cell phones. Microwaves have enough energy to heat or defrost food.

Infrared: Infrared radiation is radiating heat. If you use special goggles or cameras at night, you can see an image that shows the varying intensity of infrared radiation coming from an object, detected by heat. These waves are used by remote controls, to send signals to a device such as a TV.

Visible light: This small section of the electromagnetic spectrum is the light that we see. It has its own spectrum, ranging from red light to orange to yellow to green to blue to indigo and to violet. Lightbulbs, screens, stars, and even fireflies emit light that our eyes can detect.

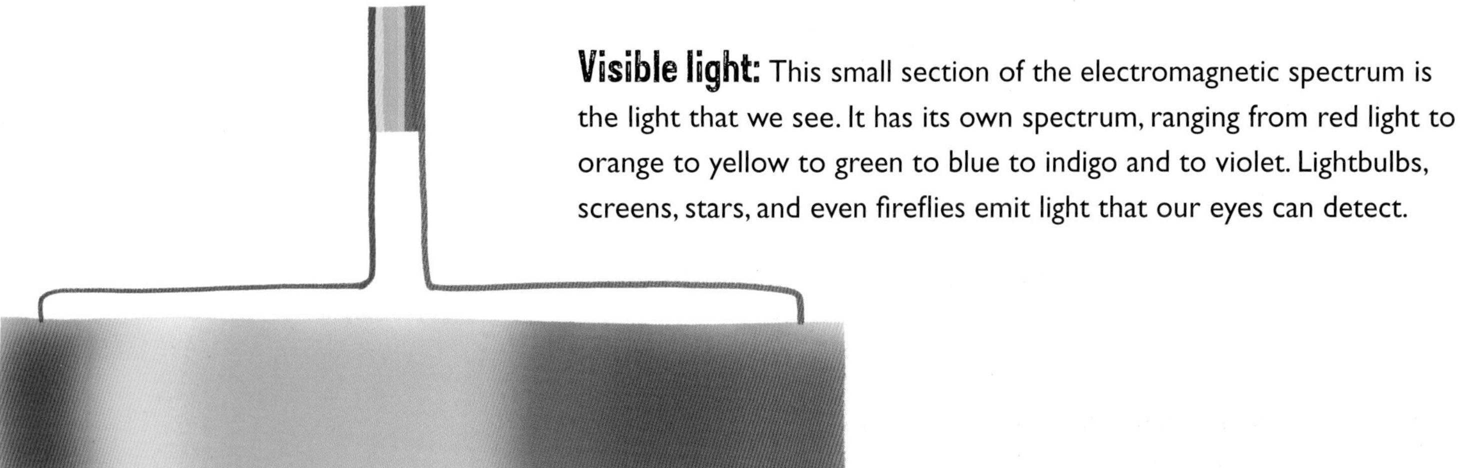

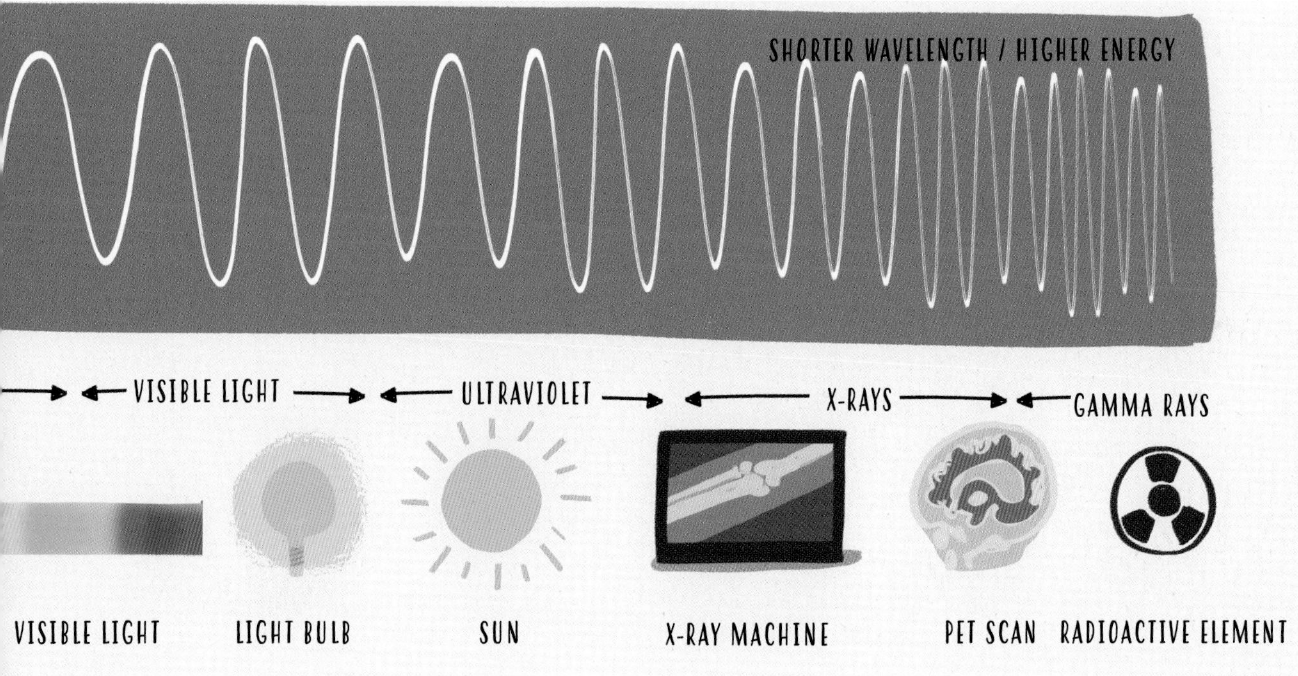

Ultraviolet: The Sun emits ultraviolet radiation—it is what can burn us! Other objects in space can also emit these waves. Some animals, such as bees, can see ultraviolet light.

X-rays: X-rays can pass through many materials that light can't. They are used by dentists to take pictures of your teeth, and by scanners at the airport to check inside bags.

Gamma rays: Gamma rays have the most energy of all. They are produced when the nuclei of radioactive materials break down. They can be used in medicine, such as to kill cancerous cells in the body.

THE MYSTERY OF LIGHT

Light is one of the wonders of the Universe. It can be invisible, yet it helps us see. It is super fast, yet it weighs nothing. So what IS it exactly? And where does it come from?

SEE THE LIGHT

Visible light is a type of energy that we can usually see, and that allows us to see the world around us. Light travels in straight lines as rays. When these rays bounce off objects and into our eyes, we can perceive the objects.

SOURCES OF LIGHT

Anything that gives off a glow of light is called a **light source**. This includes light bulbs, flashlights, fire, stars, and the Sun. The Sun is the main light source in our world. The Sun emits light all the time. It is daytime when your side of the Earth faces the Sun. When you have no sunlight, you need to find other sources of light to see what's around you.

OUT OF CURIOSITY

Stars produce heat and light in the same way as the Sun, because the Sun itself is a star. However, the Moon is different. It isn't its own light source—we can only see it when light from the Sun reflects off it.

SUN KISSED

Light sources produce light in different ways. Light bulbs and flashlights create light through electricity, while the Sun gives off natural light. The Sun and stars produce their glow from within themselves through **nuclear fusion**. The Sun is so hot that hydrogen atoms inside it smash into each other. As they do, their nuclei fuse, or join, together. This creates larger helium atoms—and releases a huge amount of energy! The energy radiates out from the Sun in all directions as heat and light. The light that arrives to Earth from the Sun includes both visible light and invisible radiation.

SHINING BRIGHT

Another form of natural light comes from living things. **Bioluminescence** is when animals emit their own light using chemical energy from chemical reactions inside their bodies. Unlike most other light sources, the energy produced by animals such as fireflies does not emit heat alongside the light. Some deep-sea fish use bioluminescence to lure in prey in the dark depths.

THE WAYS OF LIGHT

We know that light travels in waves. We also know that these waves move as rays, in straight lines. Light only changes course if it can bounce off an object and scatter in new directions.

LIGHT OR DARK

Objects look bright to us when they bounce light into our eyes. Shiny, smooth objects, such as a mirror, **reflect** most of the light they receive. Dark, solid objects **absorb** most of the light that reaches them, and so they look darker.

MIRROR IMAGE

A mirror is so smooth and shiny that the light reflects with hardly any **distortion**. This means that the reflection of an image is very clear. A pond is another reflective surface, but the ripples of water cause the light to reflect in different directions and **scatter**. Your reflection in a pond will be much more distorted and wobbly than in a mirror because of the movement of the water's surface.

REFLECTION

When light **reflects** off a smooth surface, it travels out at the same angle that it struck the object. The light ray shown here, for example, travels in a straight line until it hits the smooth, flat mirror. The ray bounces back and out at the same but opposite angle.

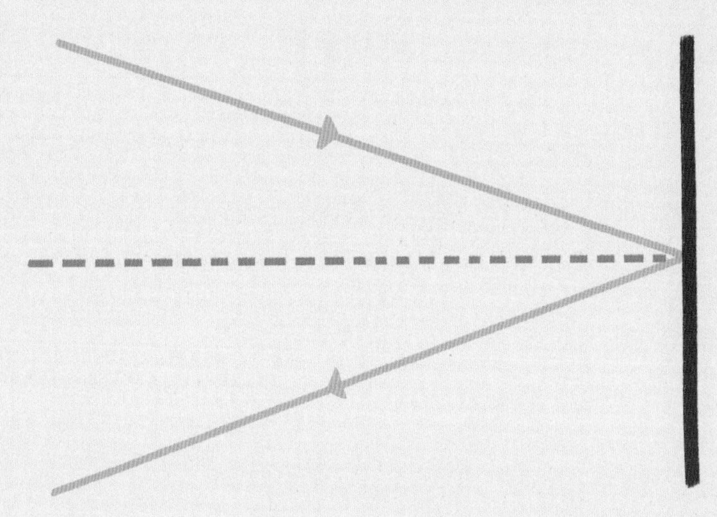

REFRACTION

When light moves from one material to another, it can look as if the light bends. This is due to **refraction**. Just as you run slower through water than you do through the air, light travels at different speeds through different materials. Think about a straw or pencil in water. The top of the pencil, out of the water, looks normal. This is because light bounces off it and into our eyes as usual. But when the light reaches the pencil in the water, the light slows down, and the bottom of the pencil looks to be in a different place.

JUST A MIRAGE

People wandering in the desert sometimes see a **mirage**. They think they see water where there isn't any! This is a trick that the light plays on their eyes. In the desert, there is a layer of very hot air just above the ground. This hot air refracts the Sun's rays, bending them back upward and creating a reflection of the sky on the sand. The brain assumes what it's seeing is water!

THE SPEED OF LIGHT

Light waves travel a million times faster through the air than sound waves. A flash of lightning reaches your eyes before the boom of thunder reaches your ears. You see the burst of fireworks before you hear the pop and sizzle. In fact, light is the fastest thing in the Universe.

TOP SPEED

If light moved only in a vacuum—empty space with nothing to slow it down—it would travel at nearly 300 million m/s (186,000 mi/s). This is the **speed of light**. How fast is that? It means that light rays from the Sun, which is about 150 million km (93 million miles) away from Earth, can reach us in just over eight minutes. Put another way, if you ran at the speed of light, you could run around Earth 7.5 times in just one second.

SPEEDY LIGHT

OUT OF CURIOSITY

Measuring things in space uses HUGE numbers. So scientists came up with using light as a measure of distance. One **light year** is the distance that light travels in one year. In these terms, the Sun is only 8 light-minutes away from us.

SPACE SHUTTLE

LIGHT

CAR

WHO WOULD WIN IN A RACE?

Spoiler alert—in a vacuum, light will always win! It is quicker than a race car, zippier than a rocket, and even faster than a speeding bullet. It travels 40,000 times faster than space shuttles, which reached speeds of 28,000 km/h (17,500 mph) to stay in orbit around Earth. It travels 10 MILLION times faster than a car on a highway.

IT'S ALL RELATIVE

Because light travels so fast, it acts in strange and unusual ways. Albert Einstein published his **theories of relativity** in the early 1900s to help explain how light behaves. **Relativity** says that how things look depends on how you are moving relative to them. When you stand on Earth, light travels in an expected way and everything looks normal. But if you could travel nearly as fast as light, time would slow down. Beyond that, if you could travel faster than light (which you can't!), time should in theory go backward.

IN THE SHADOWS

Light and shadows go hand in hand. Without light, shadows would not exist!

WHAT IS A SHADOW?

A **shadow** is simply the absence of light. It is a dark shape that occurs when an object blocks a light source. Objects can block light to different degrees.

A **transparent** object is clear, and light can pass straight through. For example, light passes through a clear glass window, and no shadow is formed.

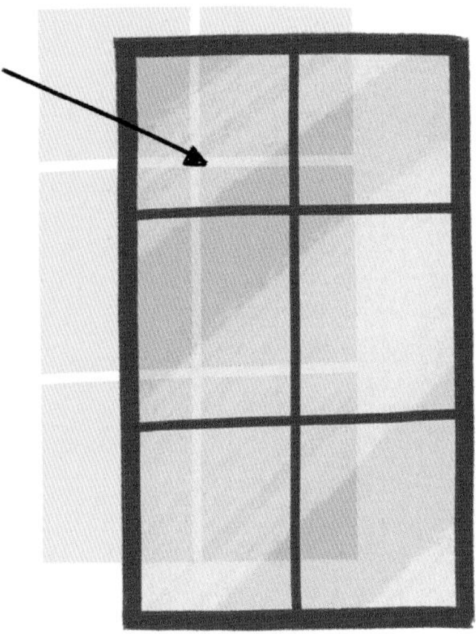

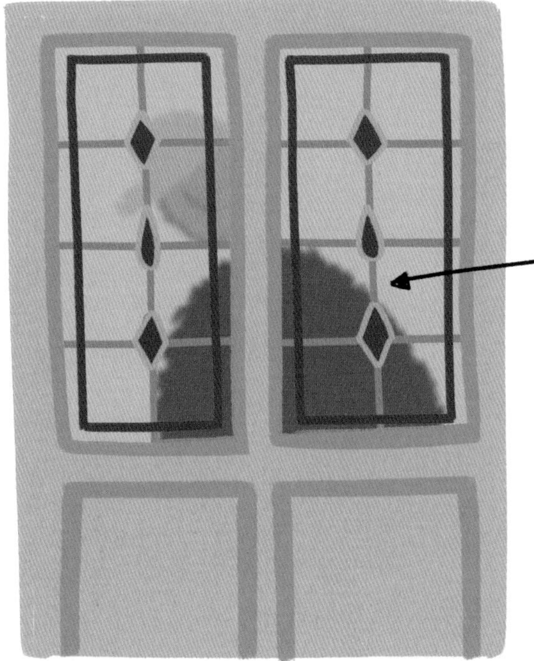

Translucent objects are semi-transparent. Light passes through, but not completely. Some light is reflected back, so objects can't be seen clearly. A frosted or stained-glass window lets light through, but you can't clearly see who's on the other side.

Opaque objects do not let light pass through them. The light is either reflected or absorbed. This means that the object blocks the light and creates a shape of darkness on the other side—a shadow.

SHADOW SHAPES

A shadow appears in the shape of the object that is blocking its light. If you place an apple between a flashlight and the wall, an apple-shaped shadow will appear on the wall. This is because the real apple blocks the light, and only the rays of light around it continue in a straight line toward the wall, leaving a dark apple shape in the middle.

Shadow **lengths** vary with the angle of the light source. A light source above an object creates a very short shadow. The lower the light source, the longer the shadow. Think of your shadow when you're outside on a sunny day. When the Sun is high in the sky, its rays shine straight down and reach most of the ground around you, so your shadow is very short. However, later in the day, when the Sun is lower in the sky, the angle makes your shadow look really long!

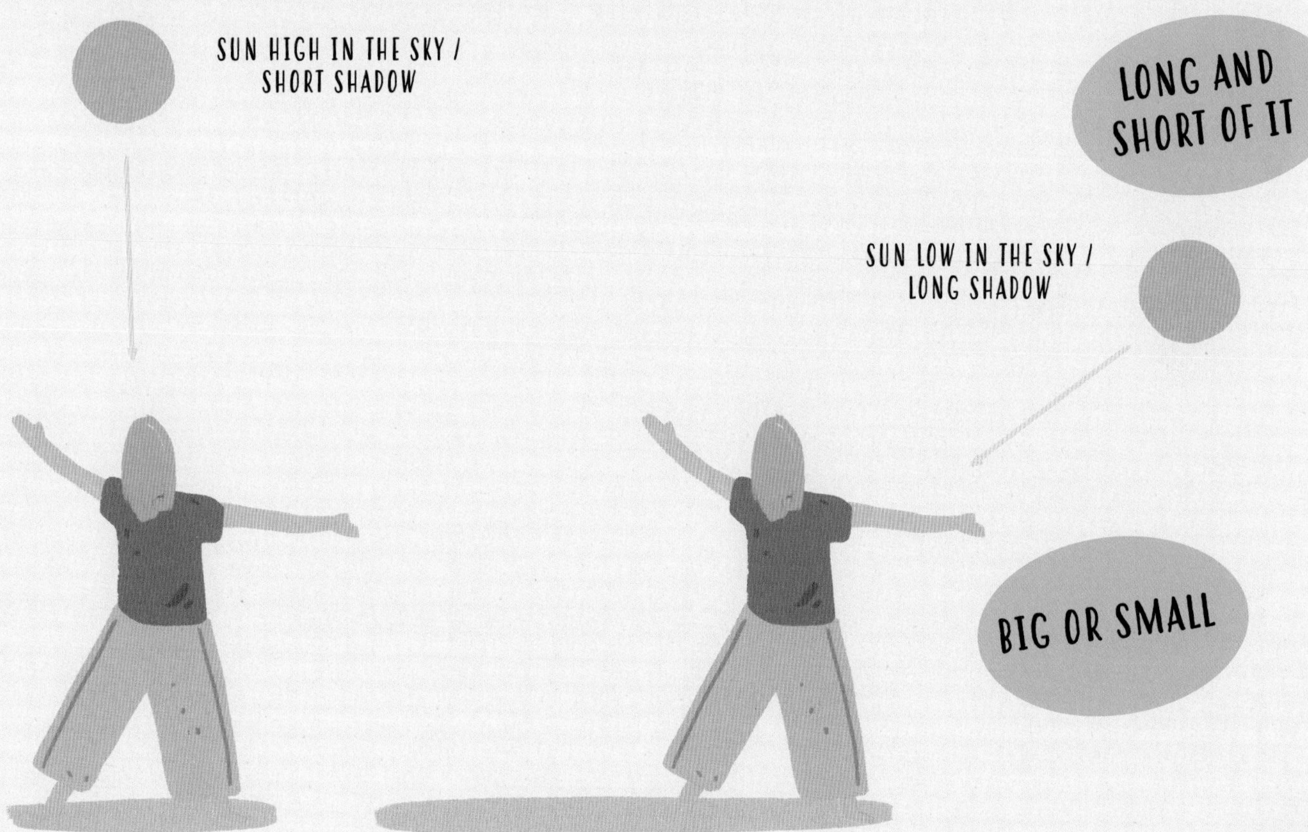

Shadow **size** can also vary. If the light source, such as a lamp, is close to the object, the shadow on the other side will be big. This is because a lot of light is blocked by the object when it's that close. But if the light source is far away from the object, the object's shadow will be much smaller, as more light can pass by it.

CREATING COLOR

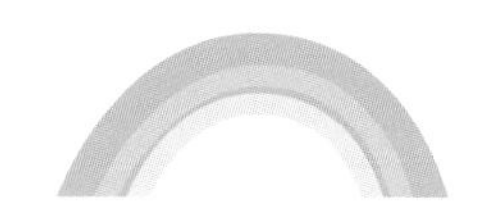

Light isn't only about the bright glow that we see from the Sun. It includes a full range of shades, which give color to our world.

WAVES OF COLOR

Visible light is part of the electromagnetic spectrum. It is made up of many colors, and each color has its own **wavelength**. Colors at the red end of the spectrum have a longer wavelength, and colors at the violet end have a shorter wavelength. The rest of the colors that we know fall somewhere in between.

WHERE COLOR COMES FROM

We see color because of the way light is reflected off objects. A white object reflects all the light that hits it. The colored waves combine to form the white that we see. White light is all the colors mixed together. A black object, on the other hand, absorbs the light and doesn't reflect any colors. Meanwhile, a yellow object absorbs all colors apart from yellow, which it reflects back into our eyes. Some colors mix together to form different shades.

CHASE THE RAINBOW

The white light of the Sun is made of every color of the rainbow. When it hits droplets of rain, the waves bend—but not all in the same way. The light reflects off the back of the raindrop and bends again as it passes back out through the front, spreading the colors out into the sky. Blue and violet wavelengths are shorter, meaning these waves have more energy, and reflect at a shallower angle than the longer wavelength colors. As the colors all reflect at their own angle, we see a rainbow form in the sky.

SUN

WHITE LIGHT

RAINDROP

OUT OF CURIOSITY

The colors of a rainbow always appear in the same order (red, orange, yellow, green, blue, indigo, violet) because of their different wavelengths.

WHY IS THE SKY BLUE?

As the Sun's rays reach Earth's atmosphere, they hit gas and dust particles. These particles reflect and scatter the different shades of the light. The shades with short wavelengths and high energy, such as blue and violet, are scattered the most and reflected into our eyes. Our eyes are more sensitive to blue than to violet, so we see a blue sky. As the Sun sets in the sky, we can see shades from the other end of the spectrum, such as red, orange, and yellow, because the rays are going through even more particles of dust and air. The blue is scattered further, allowing the other shades to shine through.

LIGHT IT UP

The light that comes from the Sun, stars, and candles is natural. To create light without relying on fire or daylight, people turned to electricity.

HOW DOES IT WORK?

A traditional light bulb has a wire inside called a **filament**. When a switch is turned on, electricity moves into the bulb and along the filament. There, the electrical energy is turned into heat and light, and the filament glows. A glass bulb around the outside protects the wire, and stops it from combining with oxygen in the air, which could make it catch fire.

Thomas Edison is known for inventing the practical light bulb that we know today. He tested thousands of different materials to use as the filament. In 1879 he created a filament out of carbon wire, which held the light's glow longer than any others he had tried before. In 1910, the chemical element **tungsten** was used, which was even more long-lasting. It is still used in many light bulbs today.

INCANDESCENT LIGHT BULBS

The original light bulbs were **incandescent bulbs**. These were any bulb with a glowing filament. The filaments were made of materials such as carbon or tungsten. Tungsten has a high melting point, which means that it can take a lot of heat without melting. However, over time, the tungsten evaporates until it burns out. To slow down this process, oxygen is removed from inside the bulb and replaced with an **inert** gas—one that does not react. This is often nitrogen or argon. Tungsten is also very fine and fragile. You must be careful not to drop these bulbs. Even if the outer glass survives the fall, the tungsten filament might break. Then the circuit is broken and the light will not glow.

HALOGEN

In a halogen light bulb, there is an extra layer of protection for the filament. A small bulb surrounding it is filled with **halogen gas**, such as iodine or bromine. As electricity passes through, it triggers something called a **halogen cycle**. Some metal evaporates from the filament, but the halogen gas returns (redeposits) so it can be reused. Halogen bulbs can last twice as long as regular tungsten light bulbs.

LED

Incandescent and halogen bulbs are not the most **energy efficient**. Most of the energy that flows through them is lost as heat. In **LED (light-emitting diodes)** lights, very little energy is lost as heat. Rather than moving along a filament, electricity passes through a material called a **semiconductor**. These bulbs may not be quite as bright as the others, but they last much longer and use a lot less power.

LIGHT AT WORK

Once you know how light works, you can make it work for you. Many inventions, from a small camera to a towering lighthouse, make use of the power of light.

LIGHT AND LENSES

A **lens** is a curved piece of glass that can bend rays of light to magnify, shrink, or focus images of objects. As the light rays pass through the lens, they are **refracted**.

CONVEX LENS

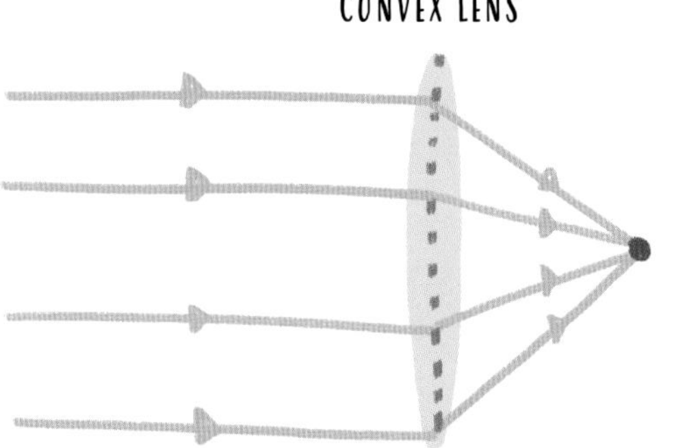

CONCAVE LENS

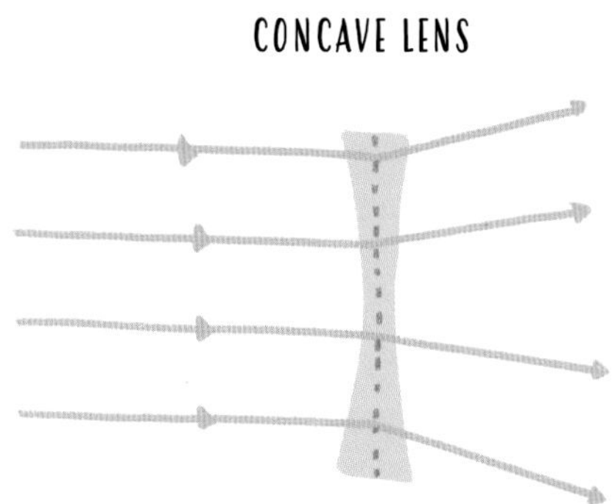

A **convex** lens is thicker in the middle than it is on the sides. Light rays that travel straight to the lens bend and **converge**, or come together, at a focal point on the other side.

A **concave** lens is thinner in the middle, and it thickens at the sides. As rays of light travel through this lens, they spread out.

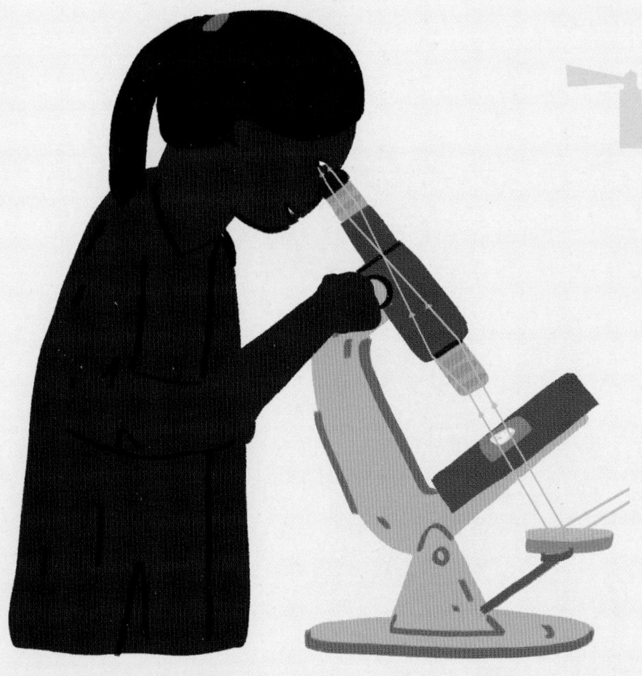

MICROSCOPE MAGIC

An **optical, or light, microscope** makes use of a series of lenses to enlarge the image of a tiny object. A mirror reflects light up through the object and into a lens, which magnifies it. The image is then magnified again by the lens at the eyepiece—where you put your eye to peer in. Optical microscopes are the most common type of microscope and can magnify objects up to 2,000 times bigger than they actually are!

TELESCOPES

Telescopes work in similar ways to microscopes. A **refracting telescope** uses a series of lenses to direct and bend light from distant objects into your eyes, at a larger size. **Reflecting telescopes** use mirrors instead of lenses to collect and direct the light from objects in space. A first, wide mirror reflects the image to another mirror, which is angled to direct the light to the eyepiece, while magnifying the image at the same time.

SAY CHEESE

A camera has a **convex** lens that focuses light into a single point. Film or a sensor captures the image. The lens focuses by changing how close it is to the object, to get the sharpest picture possible.

LIGHTING THE WAY

A lighthouse uses optics in a clever way. A large **Fresnel lens** concentrates light into a narrow, bright beam. The Fresnel lens is made of a series of **concentric** rings—one inside the other. Each ring has a lens that bends light from a light source behind. The light source shines out in all directions, but when the rays of light hit the concentric lenses, they are all directed out in straight, parallel lines—a guiding beam of light.

USING LIGHT TO SEE 

Perhaps the most important use of light in our world is the role it plays in allowing us to see. Our eyes work in a similar way to a camera, taking in pictures of the world around us for our brain to process.

HOW DOES THE EYE SEE?

Just like a camera, the eye has a **lens** that focuses light. When you look at an object in front of you, that object either emits light (such as a screen) or reflects light from another light source (such as a book under a lamp, or a tree on a sunny day). The light from the object shines or bounces into your eye through the pupil. It then passes through a **convex lens** that bends the rays toward a focus point on the **retina** at the back of the eye. This image is upside-down. Cells take the image through the optic nerve to your brain, where it is turned the right way up again.

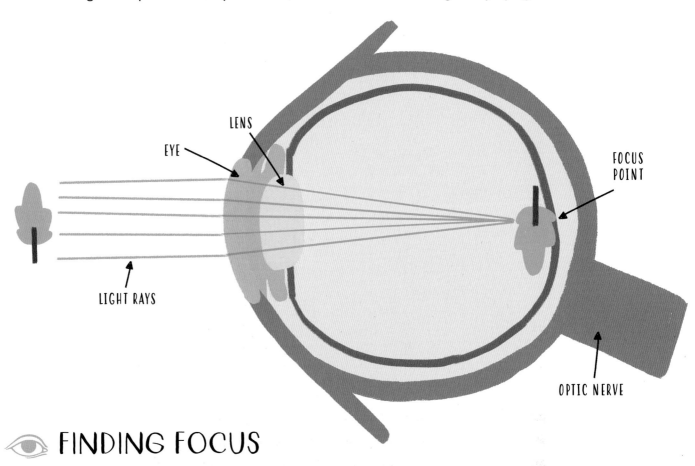

FINDING FOCUS

Tiny **muscles** in the lens can contract or relax the lens to better focus the image and angle of the refracted light. When an object is close to the eye, its light rays are more spread out. The lens squeezes to a fatter shape to bend the light rays in more sharply. When an object is far away, its rays arrive at the eye in nearly parallel lines. The lens relaxes, as it doesn't need to bend the rays quite as much.

OUT OF CURIOSITY

The lens in your eye changes shapes many times every second, so that it can go straight from focusing on your hand just in front of you, for example, to seeing the Moon, far out in space, without hesitation.

A LITTLE HELP

Sometimes, the image that appears on the retina is blurred. This can happen when the eyeball is too short or long, or if the lens muscles aren't able to focus the light rays properly. Eyesight often gets worse with age, as the muscles get weaker. **Glasses** have lenses that can help correct eyesight. Lenses are carefully designed to work with the person's individual eye lens for a sharp image for them. If a person struggles to see things close up, a **convex lens** in glasses starts to converge the rays before they reach the eye. If the person can't focus on objects far away, a **concave lens** spreads out the rays before they reach the eye.

40
50
60
70
80

CHAPTER 4

ACOUSTICS: A WORLD OF SOUNDS

The thunder that follows a flash of lightning; The music that moves from a guitar's strings to your ears; A whisper or a shout. These are all SOUND.

Acoustics is the study of sound and its properties. How can a sound be loud or quiet? High or low? How fast is sound? How do we hear? And how can we make use of sound in new and helpful ways? Listen closely to the world around you as you make your way through this noisy chapter.

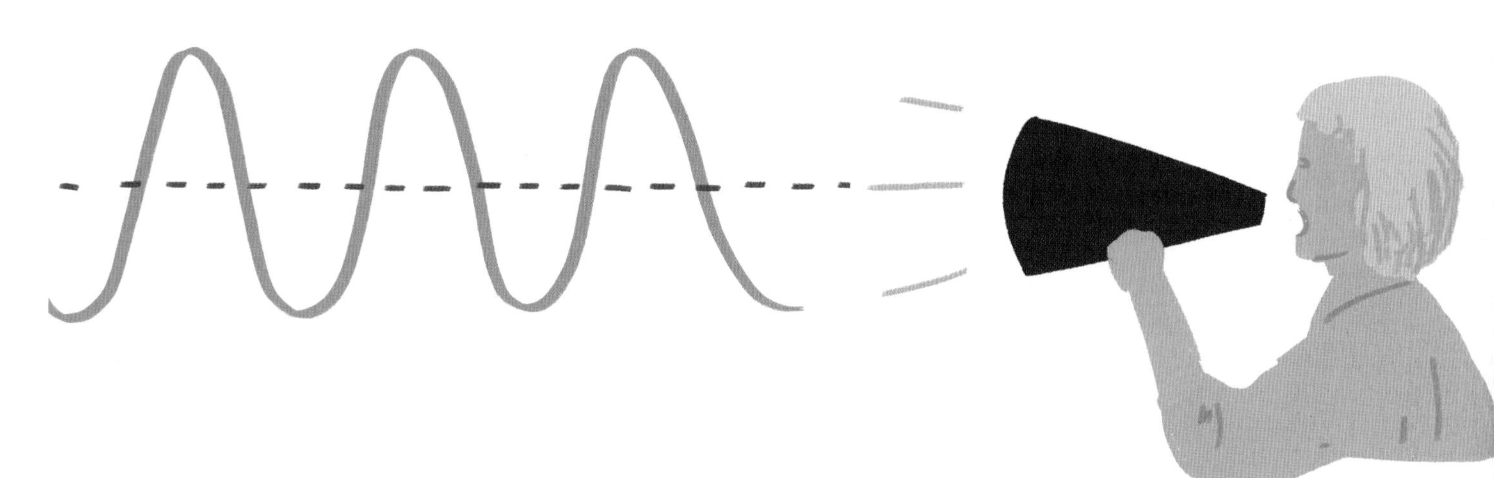

WAVES OF SOUND

If you shout in space, no one can hear you. But if you scream on Earth, you'll wake your whole house! It's all down to how sound travels.

WHAT IS SOUND?

Sound is energy that comes from **vibrations**—when things shake back and forth. When a sound is made, the vibrating object makes the air around it vibrate. This is a **sound wave**. The wave shows the pattern of changes in air pressure. Sound waves travel through the air all the way into your ear and to the **eardrum**. The eardrum vibrates and sends a message to your brain to **hear** the sound.

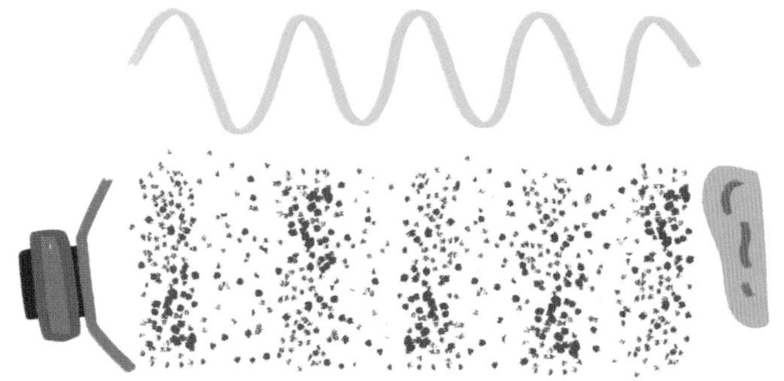

A sound wave showing the pattern of changes in air pressure

When a musician strums a guitar, the strings vibrate. These vibrations cause the air next to them to vibrate, and the sound waves travel to your ears. Your brain then recognizes these as music!

Sound waves lose energy as they travel, and the sound gets quieter along the way. Sometimes we can see the source of the sound vibrating, such as the guitar string quivering, but a lot of the time we don't see the vibrations at all. We only HEAR them.

MODE OF TRANSPORT

Sound waves need to travel through some sort of **medium**, with particles that they can cause to vibrate. They can travel through gases (such as air), liquids (such as water), and solids (such as wood or metal) ... but not in a vacuum, where there is no matter at all, such as space. In space, there are no air particles, so there is nothing for the sound to vibrate or travel on.

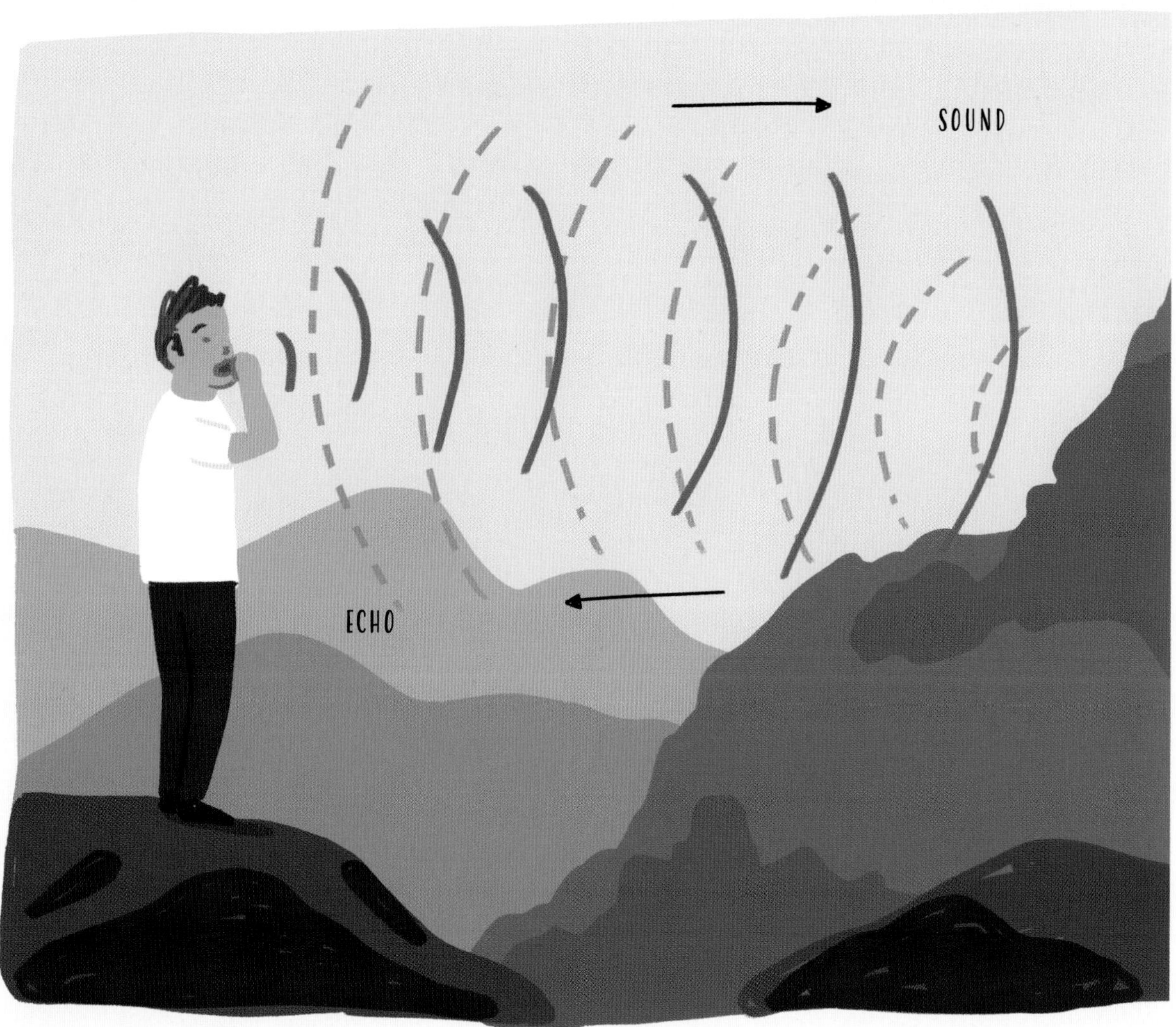

ECHO, ECHO

Just like light, sound waves can be **reflected** or **absorbed**. If a sound wave hits a soft surface, such as a cushion, it will be absorbed and the sound will disappear. But if a sound wave hits a hard, smooth object, some of it will bounce back. This is an **echo**. The sound wave reflects off the surface and carries the sound back in the opposite direction, bringing a repeat of the sound to your ears, a few moments after the original occurred. If there is another hard surface, such as in a tunnel, the sound wave will reflect again. Echo, echo! Echoes can most easily be heard where there are lots of hard surfaces, such as in caves and mountains.

VARYING VOLUME

There is a whole range of sound, from so quiet you can barely hear it to so LOUD you need to cover your ears! Sound can vary this much because of **energy**.

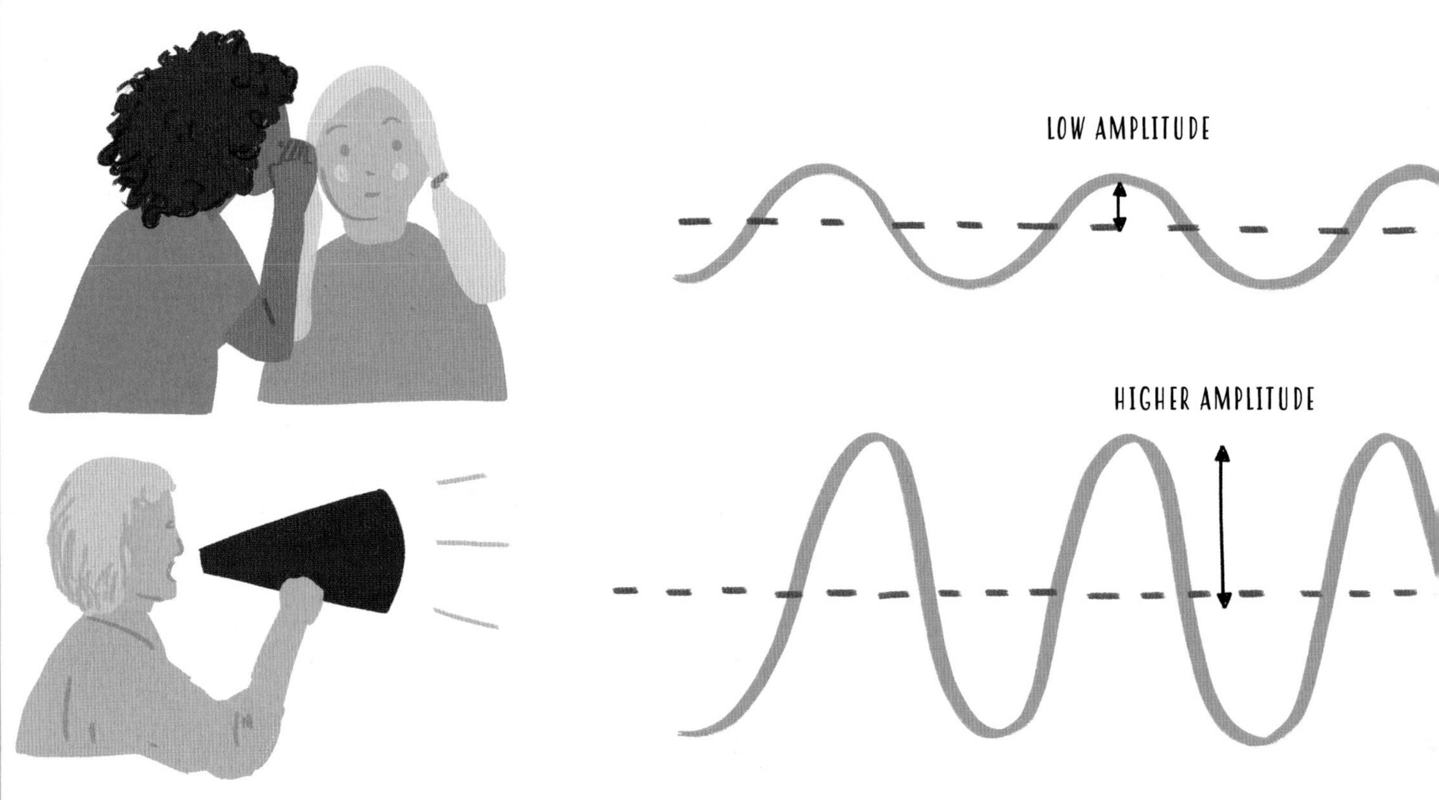

WHAT IS VOLUME?

Volume is whether something is loud or quiet. We know that sound is energy that travels in waves of vibrations, disturbing the air. The bigger and stronger the vibration, the more energy it has, and the louder sound that is produced. Bigger waves push harder against your eardrums. Smaller, weaker waves have less energy and produce quieter sounds. They don't push as hard when they enter your ear. When you whisper to a friend, you produce a quiet sound. But when you shout, the vibrations are much stronger, with more energy, and the sound is heard as loud!

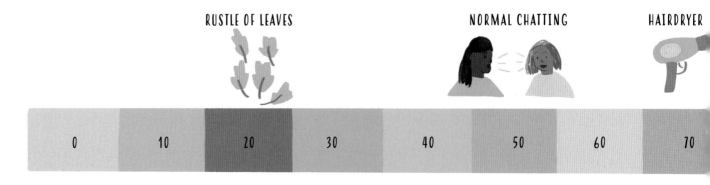

RUSTLE OF LEAVES

NORMAL CHATTING

HAIRDRYER

0 10 20 30 40 50 60 70

AMP IT UP

The height of a wave is called **amplitude**. It is measured from the middle up to the highest point in the sound wave. If you look at the wave with high amplitude, you can see it has higher peaks (the tops of the waves) and lower troughs (the dips) than the wave with low amplitude. Sounds with more energy produce more amplitude. The taller the wave, the higher the amplitude, and the louder the sound.

DISCOVERING DECIBELS

The energy of sound is measured in **decibels**. The higher the decibel level, the louder the noise. Some noises are so loud that they can damage your ears and hearing. Near the top of the decibel scale, 150 dB, is the absolute limit that our ears can take, but even before that could be damaging, depending on how close you are to the source of the sound, and how long you're exposed to it.

We can use special devices to measure decibel levels and determine how safe a sound is. These could determine whether a rock concert is too loud for its audience, or even what volume is safe to listen to your earphones.

OUT OF CURIOSITY

One of the loudest sounds ever recorded on Earth was the eruption of the Krakatoa volcano in 1883. It is estimated to have been 180 dB and could be heard 5,000 km (3,100 mi) away.

TRUCKS IN TRAFFIC

FIREWORKS OR EXPLOSION CLOSE BY

JET ENGINE

80 90 100 110 120 130 140 150 dB

PITCH PERFECT

Sound doesn't vary only by volume. It can also range in pitch.
A sound's pitch can be so high or low that our ears can't even detect it.

WHAT IS PITCH?

Pitch is how high or low a sound is. When an object vibrates and makes a sound, it can vibrate at different speeds. If an object vibrates quickly, it makes a high-pitched sound. If an object vibrates slowly, the pitch of the sound is much lower.

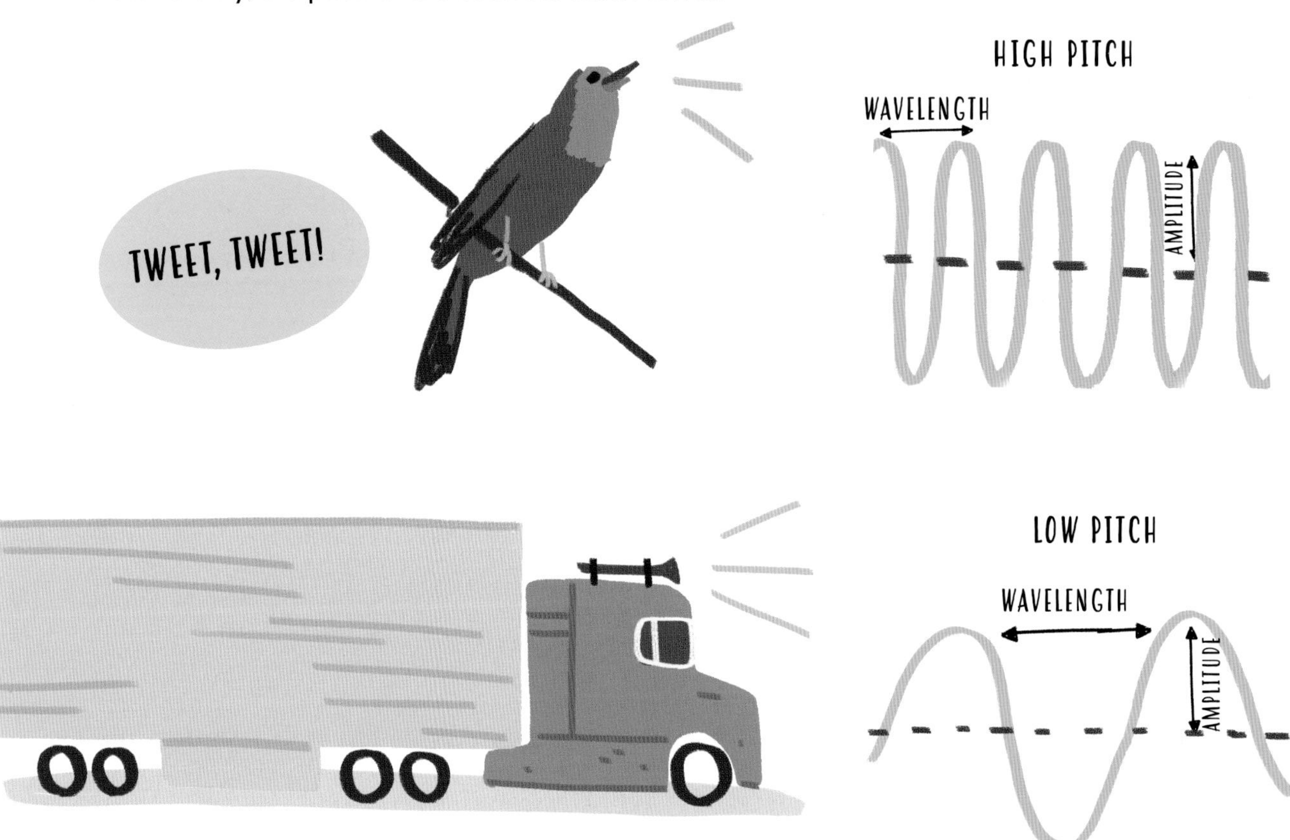

ON ANOTHER WAVELENGTH

Each sound wave has its own **wavelength**. This is the distance between the crests of two waves. The wavelengths of a high-pitched sound are short, and the waves are close together. A low-pitched sound has longer wavelengths, and the peaks are more spread out. When a bird tweets, it produces a sound that vibrates quickly. The wavelengths are close together, and the sound comes out as a high pitch. But when a truck honks its horn, the sound waves are much slower. The crests and peaks of the waves are farther apart, the wavelength is longer, and the sound comes out slow and low. Hoooonk!

FINDING FREQUENCY

Pitch is measured as **frequency**. This is the number of sound waves produced by the sound each second. It is measured in Hertz (Hz). When the waves are close together, more waves are produced in the same amount of time than when the waves are further apart. So, sounds with a short wavelength have a **high frequency** and pitch. Sounds with a longer wavelength have a **low frequency** and pitch.

A radio makes use of frequency to provide different stations. Each station has a different frequency, such as 93.9 or 100.1, which is its **waveband**. It broadcasts signals using this frequency for you to tune in.

TUNE IN!

OUT OF RANGE

Some sounds are too high or too low for our ears to detect. Sounds that are too high for our ears are called **ultrasound**. Sounds that are too low for us to hear are called **infrasound**. Some animals are able to hear sounds that we can't. A dog, for example, has ears that are more sensitive to higher frequencies. Special dog whistles can make a dog come running, while the owner can't hear the sound of the whistle at all!

HUMAN HEARING 

The human ear has many tiny parts inside that are perfectly shaped to detect sound waves.

 HOW DO WE HEAR?

When an object makes a sound, sound waves travel out from it. We know that the vibrations enter the ear, sending signals to the brain to interpret as sound. There are many stages that play a part in moving the vibrations through.

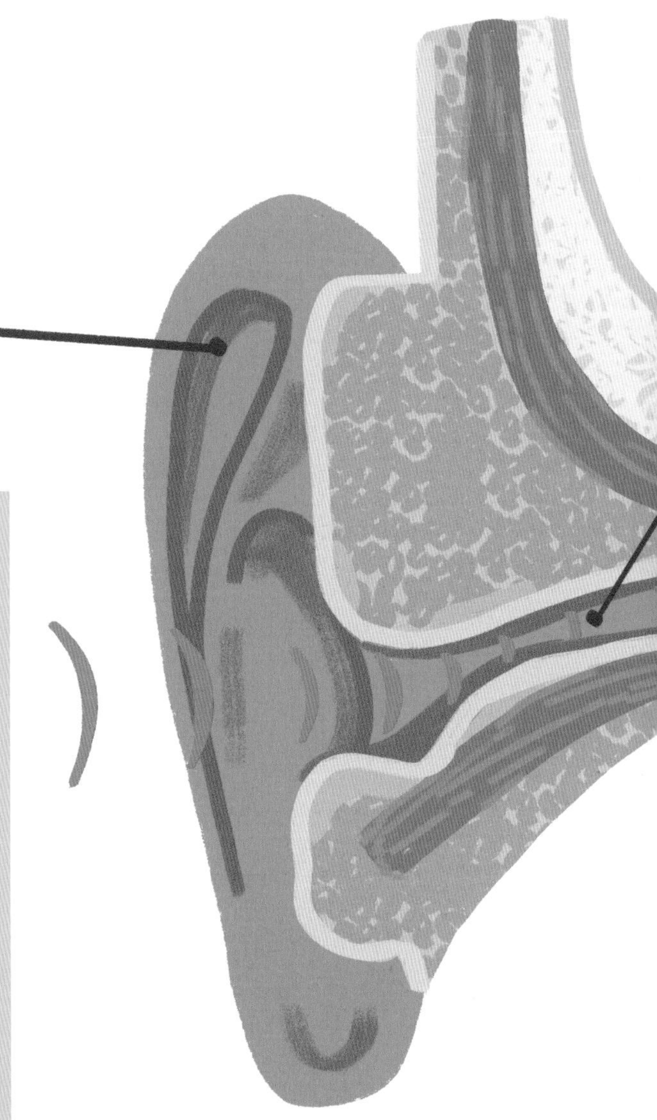

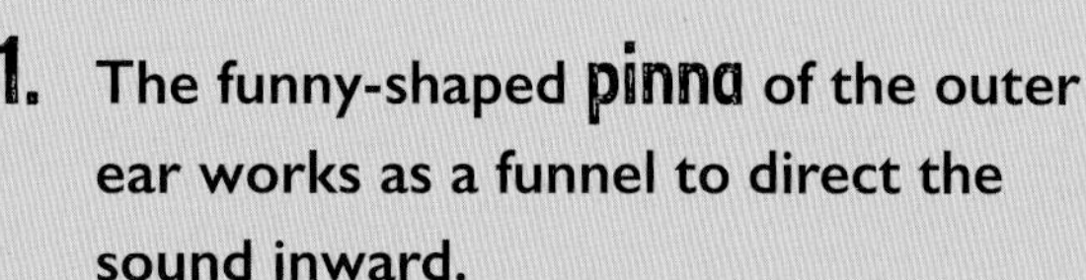

1. The funny-shaped **pinna** of the outer ear works as a funnel to direct the sound inward.
2. The sound waves travel down the tube-like **ear canal**.
3. They then reach the thin **ear drum** membrane. When they hit it, they cause it to vibrate.
4. The vibrations of the ear drum make three tiny bones, called the **ossicles**, vibrate too.
5. As the ossicles move back and forth, they push and pull on another membrane, called the **oval window**.
6. A liquid deep in tubes in the inner ear begins to vibrate. Tiny hairs in the **cochlea** pick up the liquid's vibrations and send signals to the brain to interpret the sound.

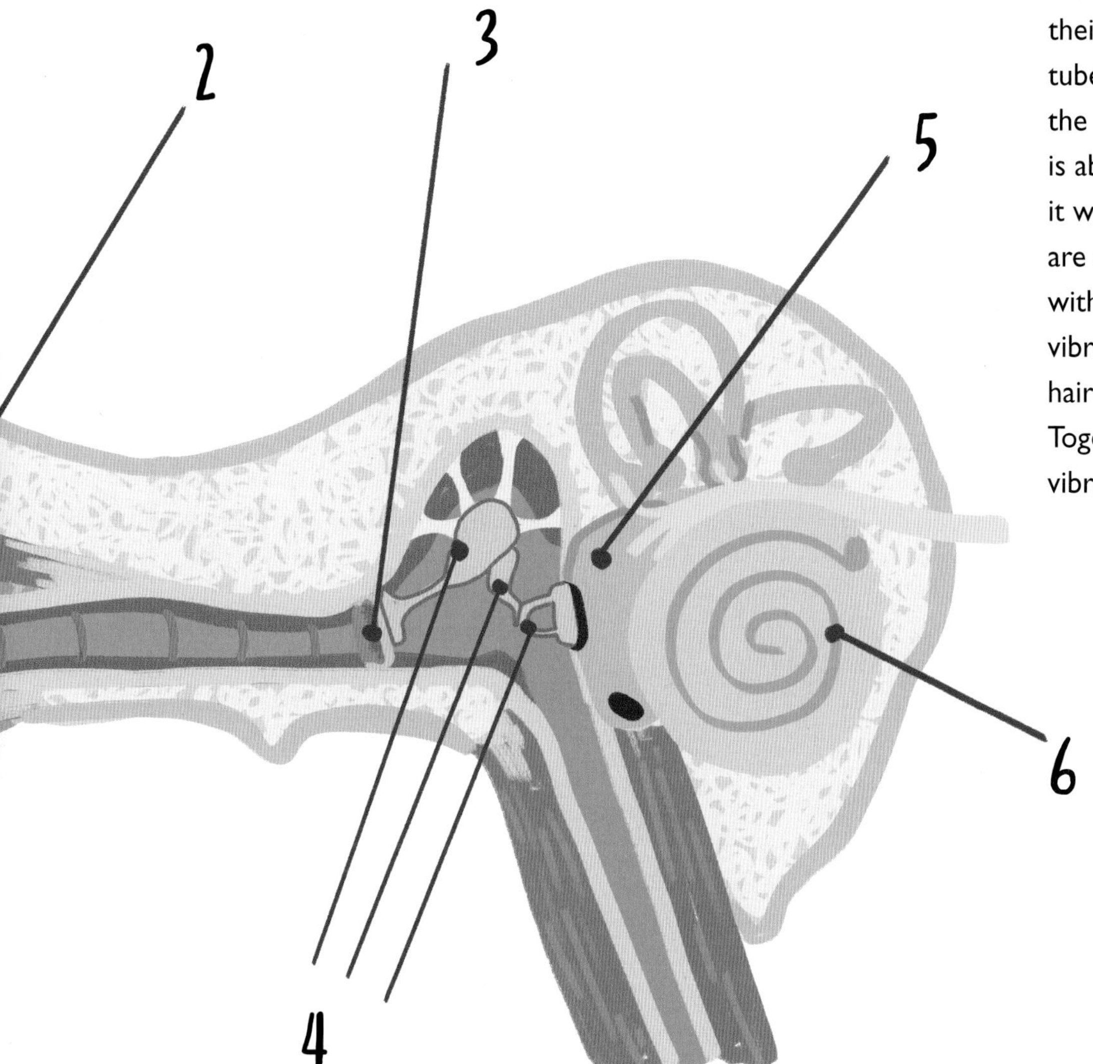

CLEVER COCHLEA

The vibrations become more and more concentrated as they go on their journey through the various tubes and membranes. By the time the sound reaches the cochlea, it is about 20 times stronger than it was outside the ear. There are about 15,000 tiny hair cells within the cochlea to pick up the vibrations in the fluid. Different hair cells pick up different sounds. Together, they pass on a pattern of vibrations to the brain.

HEARING HELP

Sometimes, this process of a sound through the ear doesn't work as it should. A person might have a burst eardrum, which can't pass on the vibrations properly. Or there might be too much fluid, or some bony growths in the ear, which disrupt the vibrations. Sometimes, a baby's ears just don't develop properly. To help with hearing, people can use **hearing aids**. A hearing aid **amplifies** sound by increasing its volume. A tiny microphone in the hearing aid detects sound around the person. The sound is converted into a digital signal. An amplifier then increases the strength of the signal, and a speaker sends that signal into the ear. Each hearing aid is made to suit an individual person's hearing loss, adjusting the volume to just the right level for them.

THE SPEED OF SOUND

Sound travels at different speeds through different mediums. It is slower than light, and some aircraft can even travel faster than it. So how fast is sound?

WHAT IS THE SPEED OF SOUND?

Sound is produced by particles vibrating. Scientists measure how quickly these particles vibrate to determine the **speed of sound**. The speed of sound varies depending on wind and temperature, but in normal air, sound travels at a speed of around 340 m (1,120 ft) per second. That means that if you made a shouting sound, it would take one second for it to reach someone standing 340 m (1,120 ft) away—the length of 40 city buses parked end to end.

FIGHTER JET – 670 M/S (2,200 FT/S)

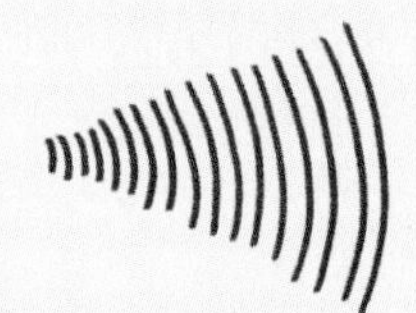

SOUND – 340 M/S (1,120 FT/S)

CAR – 134 M/S (440 FT/S)

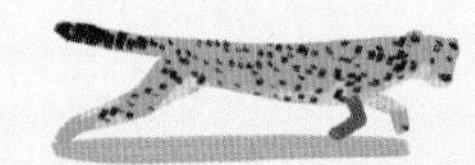

CHEETAH – 31 M/S (102 FT/S)

In the same second, a jet fighter plane can travel twice as far. It is nearly twice as fast as the speed of sound through air. However, sound through air beats both the fastest car in the world and the world's fastest land animal in a speed race.

SPEEDIER AND SPEEDIER

Sound travels faster in water than it does in air—quite a lot faster! In water, sound can travel at around 1,493 m/s (4,898 ft/s). That's over four times as fast as it travels in normal air. This is because sound travels by passing between particles. Particles in **liquids**, such as water, are closer together than they are in **gases**, such as air, so the sound can travel quicker from one particle to the next. In **solids**, such as metals, particles are even closer together, so sounds travel even faster than they do in water. In steel, for example, sound can travel at speeds of up to 5,130 m/s (16,830 ft/s)—15 times faster than in air!

NEAR OR FAR

To measure the speed of a sound, scientists can use microphones. Two microphones are placed a distance apart from the source. Scientists measure how quickly the sound travels to each one. Using the difference, they can calculate the speed of the sound.

You can also use sound to discover how far away lightning is and whether a storm is nearing or clearing. You can count the seconds between the flash that you see and the boom that you hear for each flash of lightning. If the time is getting shorter between each flash and boom, then the storm must be getting closer. But if the time between each flash and boom is longer each time you count, then the storm must be moving farther away. However close or far, make sure you stay safe inside!

GOING SUPERSONIC

Some objects can travel faster than sound in air. When they do, they can create incredible shock waves and sounds.

FASTER THAN THE SPEED OF SOUND

The speed that sound particles travel through normal air—340 m (1,120 ft) per second—is known as **Mach 1**. If something travels faster than Mach 1, it is called **supersonic**. It is faster than the speed of sound.

BOOM!

SONIC BOOM

As a jet plane flies, its engines make sound waves that spread out in all directions. The jet plane eventually moves faster than the sound particles and passes in front of them. As the plane catches up with its own sound waves, it squashes these waves together. This creates a huge sound called a **sonic boom.** On the ground, you might hear this as a loud sound a bit like thunder sweeping past you.

SHOCK WAVE

A **shock wave** is a sharp change in pressure that occurs when something passes the speed of sound. We can see this as a cone-shaped cloud. As a plane nears supersonic speeds, it squashes the air particles in front of it closer together. Behind the aircraft, the particles of air spread out, and the temperature cools. With the cooler temperature, any water in the atmosphere condenses into droplets. Behind the jet, this water vapor spreads out into a cone shape. Eventually, it disappears as the air particles return to normal.

TOO LOUD!

Aircrafts that travel faster than the speed of sound are normally fighter jets. Most commercial planes that you take to travel from place to place don't reach these speeds, so you won't hear a sonic boom. However, private jets are getting faster and faster—but they are limited by the sound of reaching Mach 1. A sonic boom can be considered too much noise impact for the environment, and so scientists and engineers are working hard to find ways to muffle the sound.

OUT OF CURIOSITY

Concorde was the first passenger-carrying commercial plane to fly at supersonic speeds. It could reach a speed over Mach 2—twice as fast as the speed of sound. It operated from the 1970s until 2003, when it went out of service due to the high costs of running it, and the noise.

MAKING MUSIC

Some sounds, like the scratching of nails on a chalkboard, can make you shudder. Others, such as a siren close by, can make you cover your ears! But music is sound that is pleasant to listen to.

WHAT IS MUSIC?

Music comes from sounds that are combined to be pleasing to the ear. Music is so powerful that it can make you want to dance, smile, or even cry. It is made from sound vibrations created on different **instruments**. Series and patterns of these sounds travel to your ears, and the brain interprets them as **music**.

MUSICAL NOTES

Many instruments can be **tuned** to different frequencies. Each string on a guitar, for example, can be tuned differently to create a variety of frequencies for the guitar, ranging from high to low pitches. These are called **musical notes**. Different instruments can play the same musical notes, by playing the same frequency, but the sound will come out differently due to the sound waves created by the different types and shapes of the instruments. Bigger instruments, such as the cello, tend to produce loud, low notes, for example. Tiny instruments such as the piccolo will only play notes of higher frequencies.

WIND

Wind instruments make music from the air itself vibrating. The musician blows into the instrument to make the air inside vibrate, such as on a flute or recorder, or blows across a small reed on a clarinet or oboe. Keys on the instruments can be pressed or released, opening different holes for the air to exit. Blocking different holes creates different pitches and notes.

PERCUSSION

Percussion instruments are ones that you strike with your hand or a stick, such as the drums, triangle, bell, and xylophone. On a drum, a skin is pulled tightly across the top. When the skin is struck, it vibrates up and down to produce sound. A bell or xylophone is made of metal that vibrates and moves the air around it.

STRINGS

Instruments such as the guitar, violin, cello, and harp are called **stringed** instruments. Strings are pulled tightly across the instrument, and pegs can be tightened or loosened to tune them to a specific frequency. The strings vary in thickness to allow a range of possible frequencies. Thicker strings make lower pitched notes and thinner strings make higher notes. When you strum a guitar string, or run a bow across a string on a violin, the string vibrates. The sound echoes out of **sound holes** in the instrument, to project the sound out and toward your ears.

THE DOPPLER EFFECT

Waves change with movement. They can bunch up around objects, and spread out too. This fact has fascinating effects on sound, as well as on our understanding of the great big Universe.

WHAT IS THE DOPPLER EFFECT?

The **Doppler effect** is the change in frequency of sound or light waves depending on the sound or light's relative position and motion to the listener. Think about the siren noise you hear as a flashing ambulance rushes past you. As it approaches, the sound is high-pitched. But as soon as the ambulance passes, the sound becomes lower—weeeee-oooh. This is because of the siren's sound waves. As the ambulance approaches you, its sound waves bunch together, just like water waves in front of a duck swimming forward. This gives the ambulance's sound waves a shorter wavelength and a higher pitch. But as it leaves you, the sound waves behind are stretched. The wavelength increases, giving the sound a lower pitch.

TRUMPETS ON A TRAIN

In 1845, scientists tested the Doppler effect on a steam train. Musicians on a train played and held the same note as the train passed through a station. Observers standing on the station platform measured the pitch and confirmed that, sure enough, it lowered as soon as the train passed them.

PROOF IN THE LIGHTING

The Doppler effect applies to light as well as sound. With light, this can be seen by a change in shade. As stars move closer to Earth, they have a shorter wavelength and look bluer. And as stars move farther away, they appear redder due to their longer wavelength. This is called **redshift**. When using a special telescope, scientists can see that most stars in our Universe appear red, rather than blue. This shows that they—and their galaxies—are moving away from us. This is proof that the Universe is expanding.

OUT OF CURIOSITY

The Doppler effect is named after physicist Christian Doppler. He was born in Austria in 1803 and studied mathematics, physics, and astronomy. He was fascinated with the varying shades of stars and discovered the Doppler effect in 1842.

DOPPLER TODAY

Since its discovery, the Doppler effect has been used in different ways. In the 1940s, Doppler radar was developed. This helped read and predict weather, such as the position of storms, more accurately by taking into account shifts from the Doppler effect. In 1999, astronomers discovered that stars were even farther away than they thought. This means that the Universe is not only expanding, but it's expanding quicker and quicker too!

SOUND AT WORK

Sound is everywhere in our world. Knowing how it travels, and how quickly, can help with important technology. Animals in the wild make use of sound too.

SONAR

Ships and submarines can measure depth and distance in the ocean using sound. A device called SONAR (Sound Navigation and Ranging) sends out sound waves. The sound waves travel through the water and bounce off the bottom of the ocean, or another object such as an iceberg. They return to the device as an echo. By measuring how long this echo takes to return, we know how far away the object or bottom of the sea is. In deep, dark water, it is hard to see icebergs, so detecting them using sound helps submarines avoid a crash.

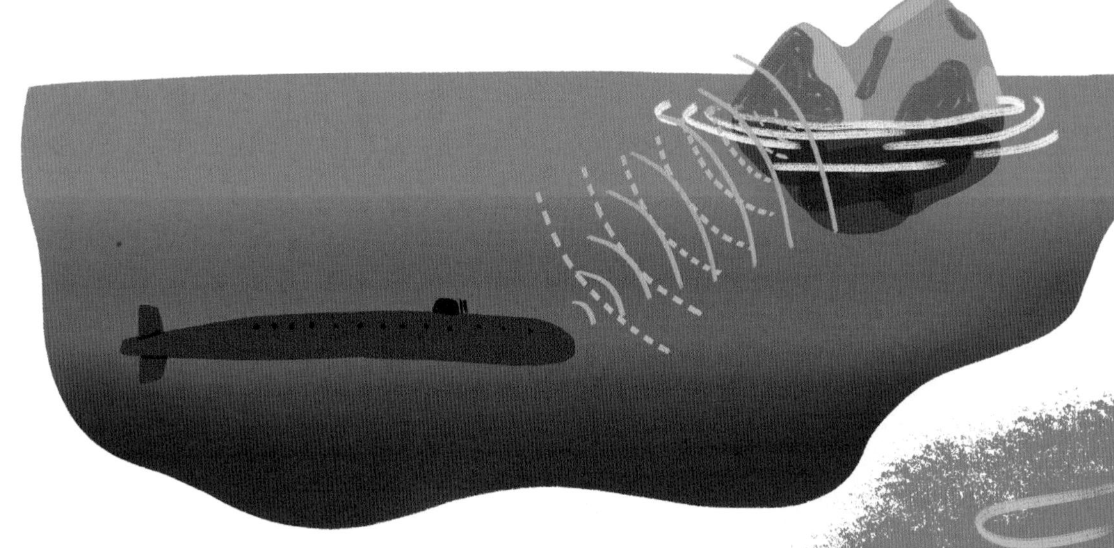

ECHOLOCATION

Animals such as dolphins, whales, and bats use a similar system to find prey. These animals hunt in the dark, or the deep, so they can't easily see food in front of them. Instead, they rely on their sense of hearing. The animals send out a series of high-pitched clicking sounds. The sound waves bounce off prey, such as fish or insects, and echo back to the very sensitive ears of the dolphin or bat. The hunter listens for the echo to determine where it's coming from—and then it pounces.

ULTRASOUND

Ultrasound is the high-pitched sound that is too high for our ears to detect. Instead of using it to hear, we use it to see. A common use of ultrasound is in medical scanning. Doctors send ultrasound waves into a pregnant mother's body to check on the development of her baby. The waves reflect off the baby inside and bounce back to a receiver. The sound waves are put together in an image on a computer screen. Hello, baby!

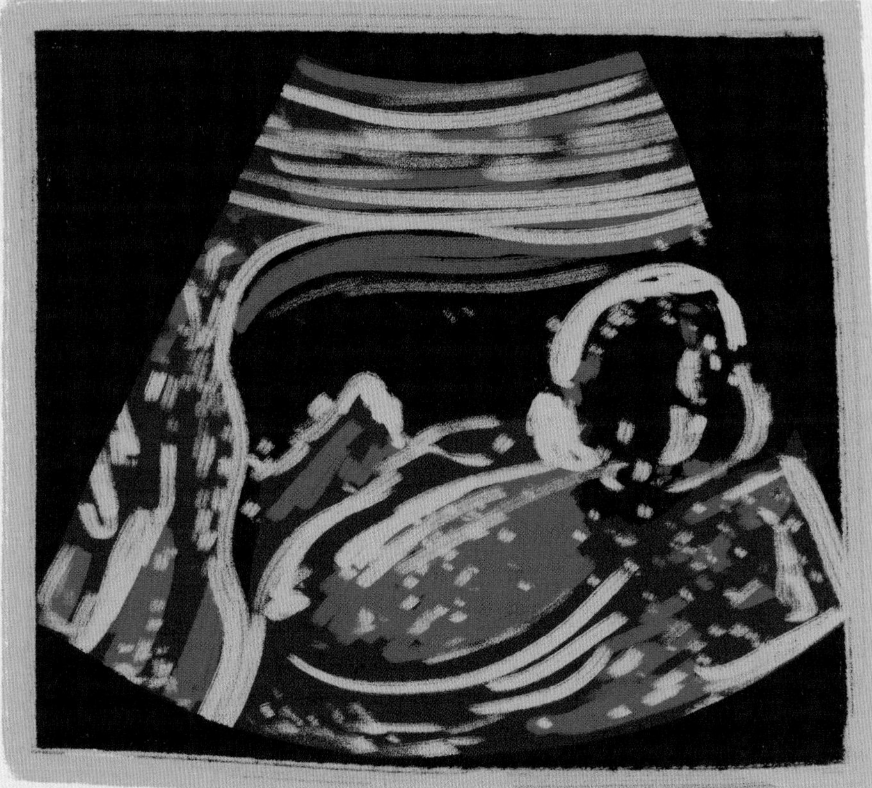

Ultrasound can also be used for **cleaning** metals such as rings. A ring is placed in an ultrasound bath, where the fast, high-pressure vibrations of the ultrasound waves shake the dirt right off.

SHAKE IT OFF!

OUT OF CURIOSITY

Along with making sounds to detect location and prey, whales use songs to communicate and look for mates. Their low pitches can travel far through the water.

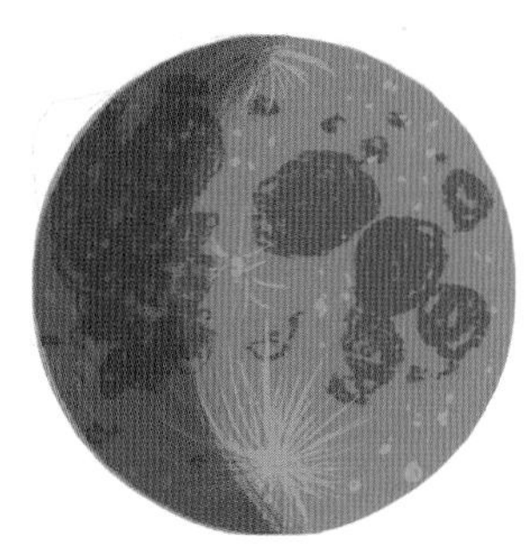

CHAPTER 5

ASTROPHYSICS: JOURNEY INTO SPACE

We know that space is full of stars, planets, the Sun, the Moon ... But how? Where did the Universe begin, and how does our Solar System stay in place? In this chapter, we will look at the PHYSICS of space.

Astrophysics is the study of the stars and other objects in space, and how the laws and theories of physics can explain our Universe. This includes orbits, tides, seasons, and even space travel. Strap in, and prepare for an out-of-this-world ride.

IT BEGAN WITH A BANG

It all started with a bang—the Big Bang that created the Universe itself. From there, energy, matter, stars, planets, and the world that we know eventually came to be.

MAGICAL MOMENT

In a fraction of a second, 13.7 billion years ago, the Universe was created by what we call the **Big Bang**. Space-time burst into existence and expanded incredibly rapidly. A tiny point exploded, and it has continued to expand ever since. That moment created all the energy and matter that exists in our Universe.

TIMELINE OF THE UNIVERSE

In the beginning, the Universe was very dense and very hot.

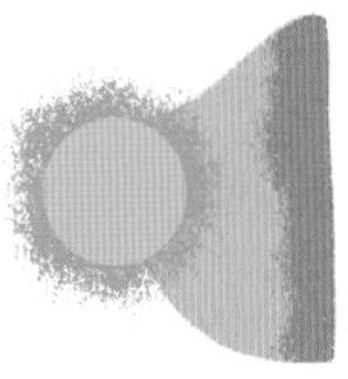

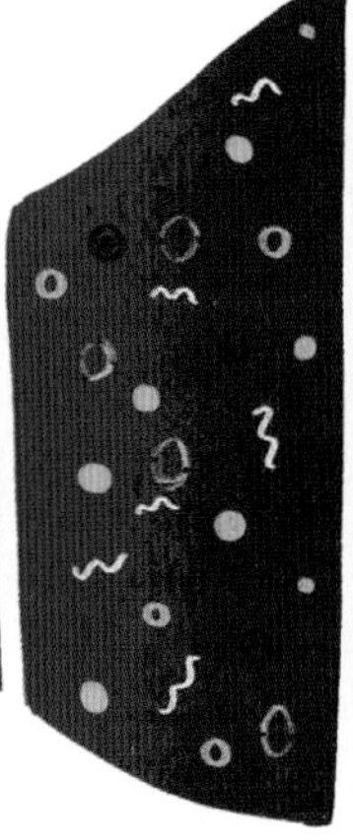

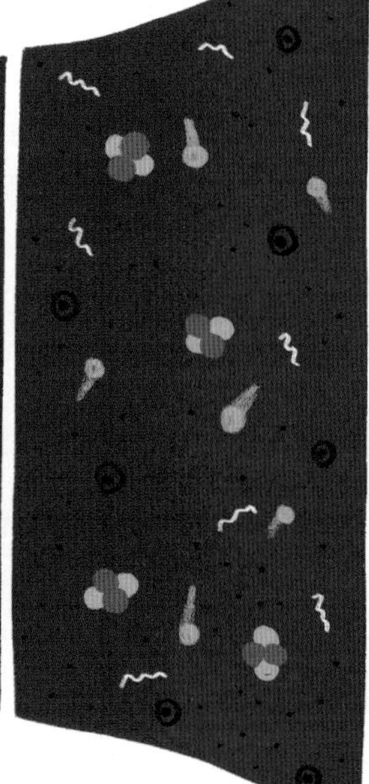

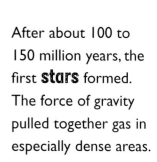

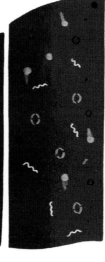

Within the first second, it grew from a teeny-tiny point to bigger than the size of a city. It then continued to expand, but at a slower rate.

The energy of the explosion created **matter**.

Neutrons and protons began to form. The Universe was still too hot for atoms to exist, but some of their pieces were there.

After 380,000 years, the Universe cooled down enough for **atoms** to form. Protons and neutrons were joined by electrons. The Universe became a swirling cloud of gases.

After about 100 to 150 million years, the first **stars** formed. The force of gravity pulled together gas in especially dense areas.

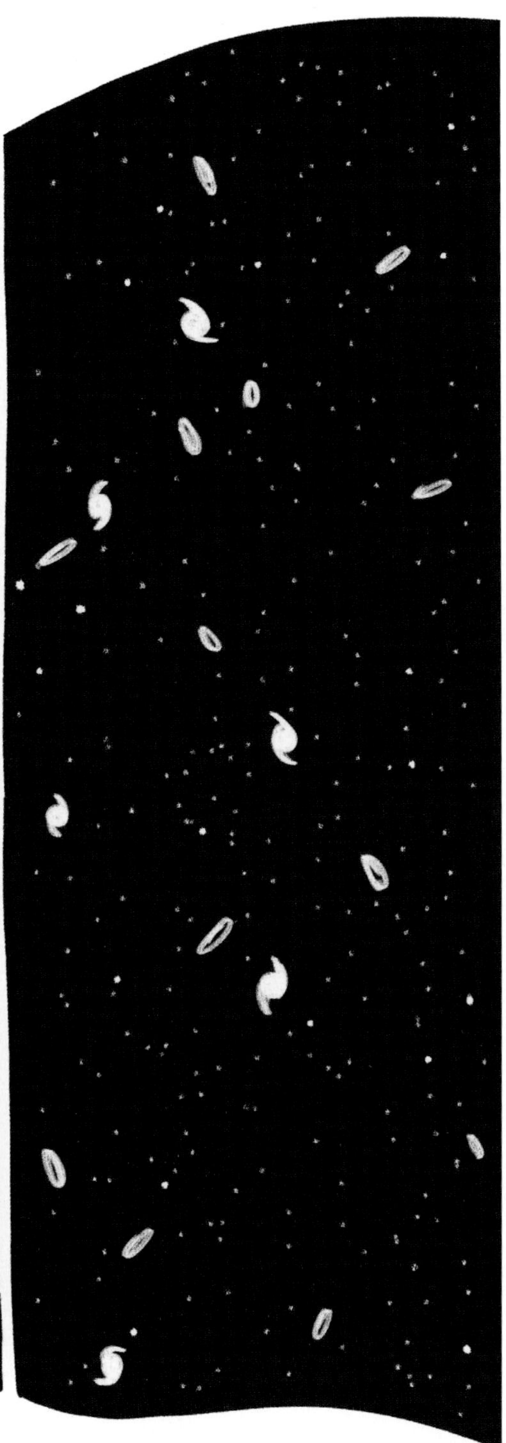

After a few hundred million years, **galaxies** formed. Gravity pulled groups of stars together into spinning clusters.

Today, the Universe has stars, galaxies, planets, moons—and living things like us. It is still expanding and seems to have no outer limits.

LEMAITRE AND HUBBLE

The first person to suggest the Big Bang was Belgian astronomer Georges Lemaître. In 1927, he proposed that the Universe was expanding. Four years later, he went on to suggest that the Universe had begun with a tiny point, which he called the "cosmic egg." In 1929, American astronomer Edward Hubble discovered that galaxies were moving farther away. This supported Lemaître's expansion theory. There was plenty of resistance to these ideas, but after several decades their theories were proven to be correct.

LINGERING PROOF

Radiation from the Big Bang still exists in our Universe today. Using special telescopes, scientists can see this cosmic microwave background radiation (CMBR), which is yet more proof of the journey of the Universe from hot to cool and tiny to huge.

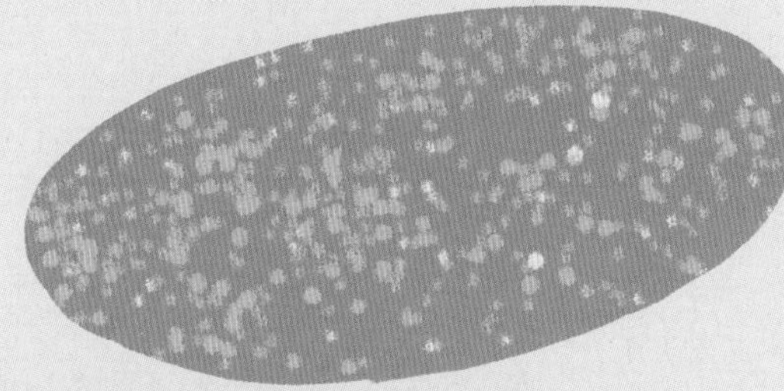

OUT OF CURIOSITY

The name "Big Bang" was given to this event not by someone who supported the theory—but by someone who opposed it! In 1949, astronomer Fred Hoyle said, "This big bang idea seemed to me to be unsatisfactory..." And the name stuck!

 OUR PLACE IN SPACE 

The Solar System is the group of planets and other objects that travel around a central star—our Sun. It has been around for BILLIONS of years.

THE BIRTH OF THE SOLAR SYSTEM

The Solar System began to form about 4.6 billion years ago from a cloud of gas and dust. Gravity pulled the gas and dust together into a star, creating a dense core. As atoms of gas were forced closer and closer together, the temperature and pressure increased until the nuclei of hydrogen atoms crushed together and **fused**. This process created helium and continues to do so in the Sun today, releasing a whole lot of energy and keeping it hot.

Over 10 million years, this star became our Sun. Matter that wasn't drawn in to the Sun came together through the pull of gravity and formed planets, asteroids, or comets.

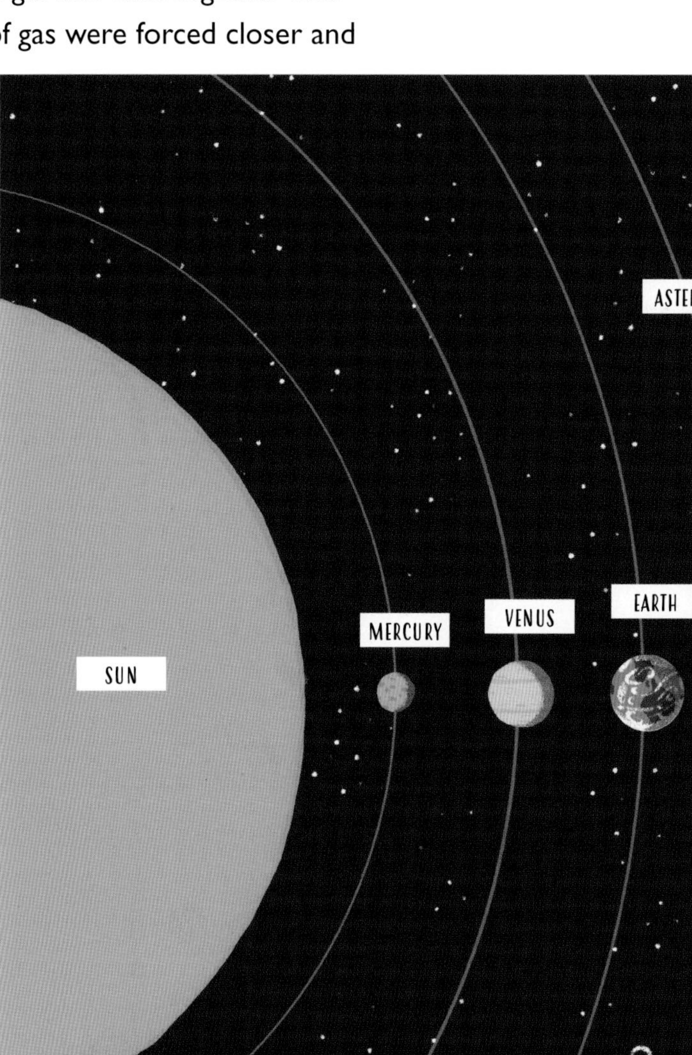

 THE PULL OF THE SUN

The Sun is the largest object in our Solar System. It has such a strong gravitational pull that it draws all the other objects toward it. Each of these objects **orbits** around the the Sun, at its own distance.

PLANET POWER

While planets orbit the Sun, they also have their own **gravitational pull.** This holds them in a sphere shape. It also pulls objects around the planets in to orbit, such as moons.

There are eight planets in our Solar System. The four planets closest to the Sun—Mercury, Venus, Earth, and Mars—are called **rocky planets** because they are made up of mainly rock and metal. They are denser than the outer planets.

The outer planets are less dense and much bigger. They are made mainly of gas and liquid around a smaller rocky core. These four outer planets—Jupiter, Saturn, Uranus, and Neptune—are called the **gas planets**. Jupiter and Saturn are called **gas giants**. Uranus and Neptune are the farthest planets from the Sun. They are cold **ice giants**.

JUPITER
SATURN
URANUS
NEPTUNE

GALAXY QUEST

The Universe is full of billions, or possibly even trillions, of galaxies. Each galaxy is a group of stars held together by gravity. Our Solar System lives in the **Milky Way**. The Milky Way is a **spiral galaxy**. All the stars, planets, and dust swirl around a central nucleus—supermassive black hole. It takes about 250 million years for our Solar System to travel all the way around.

BURNING BRIGHT

When you look outside on a clear night, you can see twinkling stars filling the sky. In fact, the Universe is full of stars of different types and ages.

WHAT IS A STAR?

A star is a giant ball of hot gas. It is made of mainly helium and hydrogen, pulled and held together by the force of gravity. Just like the Sun (which is also a star), stars burn and shine through the process of **nuclear fusion**. This process releases a whole lot of heat and light energy.

THE LIFE OF A STAR

Most stars are born inside dense clouds of gas and dust called **nebulas**. When something disturbs a nebula, it begins to collapse inward under gravity. Areas in the cloud pull in matter, and the nebula collapses around these points. Each of these draws into a ball shape and continues to shrink and heat up. When the core reaches about 10 million °C (18 million °F), nuclear fusion occurs and we have a star.

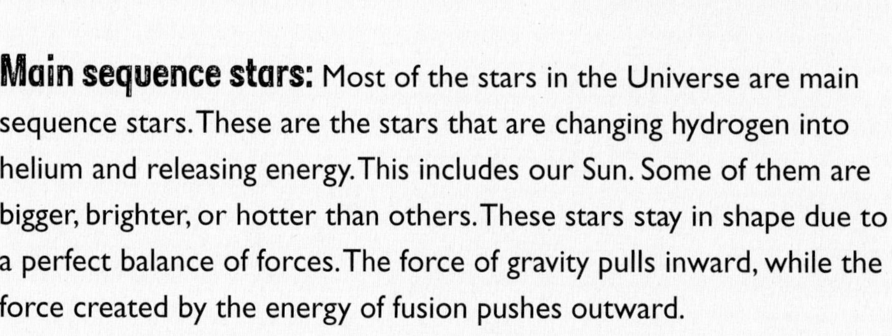

Main sequence stars: Most of the stars in the Universe are main sequence stars. These are the stars that are changing hydrogen into helium and releasing energy. This includes our Sun. Some of them are bigger, brighter, or hotter than others. These stars stay in shape due to a perfect balance of forces. The force of gravity pulls inward, while the force created by the energy of fusion pushes outward.

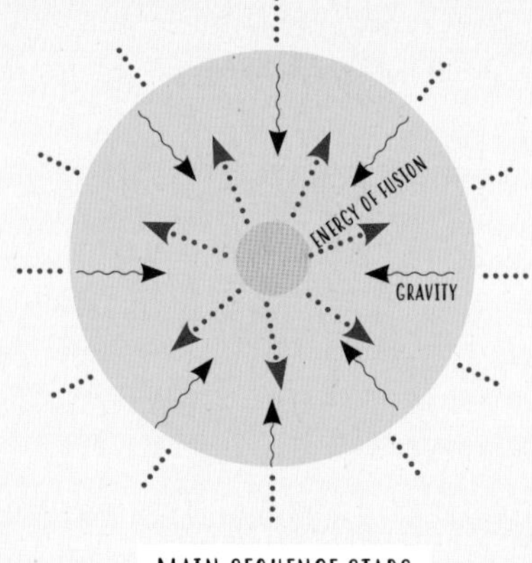

MAIN SEQUENCE STARS

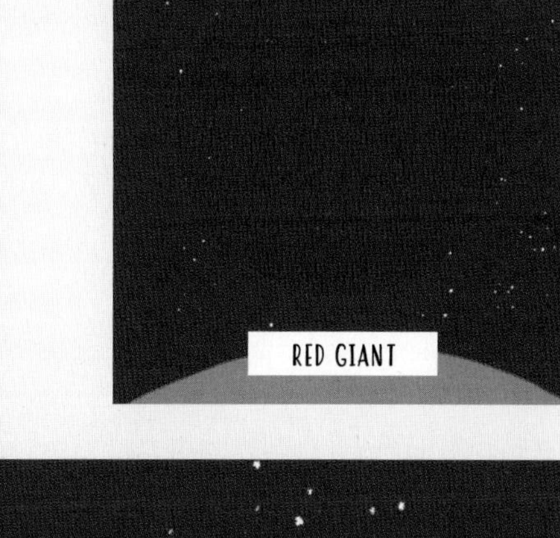

Red giant: When a star with a similar mass to our Sun begins to run out of hydrogen in its core, it becomes a red giant. These stars aren't releasing the same heat energy as before, so they are cooler than main sequence stars, giving them a red shade.

White dwarf: Eventually, the red giant stops nuclear fusion. The core collapses, and the star is left as a tiny, hot, dense spot with a faint glow that lasts for billions of years.

Supergiant: A supergiant is the largest type of star in the Universe. Supergiants burn through their hydrogen quickly and can give off a million times more energy than the Sun. They burn out quickly in star terms, within just a few million years.

Supernova: Instead of shrinking quietly into a white dwarf, when a supergiant runs out of fuel, it explodes! The core of the star collapses suddenly and heats up. This creates an explosion that blasts the outer layers of the star into space. The inner core then becomes a small neutron star or a black hole.

WHY DO STARS TWINKLE?

Stars emit light rays that travel outward. They are so far away that the beams reaching Earth are very thin. When they hit Earth's atmosphere, which is full of moving air, they bend. We see this as the star twinkling—even though it isn't. Planets are much closer to Earth, so they shine more steadily. You can pick them out in the night sky as the dots that don't twinkle.

SPREADING SUNSHINE

Without the Sun, our Solar System would not exist. It keeps all the other planets in place, and it heats Earth to just the right temperature for living things to make a home.

WHAT IS THE SUN?

The Sun is a main sequence star. It is a spinning ball of hot, glowing gas, continuously burning through the process of **nuclear fusion**. This process releases energy in the form of heat and light. The Sun's energy reaches all eight planets in our Solar System. By the time it reaches the outer planets, it is much weaker, so these planets are colder and darker than the inner four. The sunshine emitted is a mix of types of **electromagnetic radiation**, including visible light, infrared (which we experience as heat), and UV. Earth's atmosphere mostly protects us from any harmful radiation (and sunscreen does too!).

OUT OF CURIOSITY

The Sun's core is about 15 million °C (27 million °F). Just its surface temperature is hot enough to boil a diamond!

FORCE FROM THE SUN

The Sun is the largest object in our Solar System by far. In fact, it makes up over 99% of the mass of the entire system. You could fit a million Earths inside it! Because it is so massive, the Sun's **gravity** is extremely strong. It holds the Sun in its ball shape, and it pulls every other object in the Solar System into orbit around it. This includes eight planets, at least five dwarf planets, thousands of asteroids, and trillions of comets and pieces of ice.

The Sun also produces a **magnetic** force. Electric currents inside it generate a magnetic field. This is carried through the Solar System on solar wind—a stream of electrically charged gas particles that blow out from the Sun in all directions. The solar wind travels extremely fast through space. Luckily, Earth has its own magnetic field surrounding it. This deflects the solar wind away from our planet.

IT'S MAGNETIC!

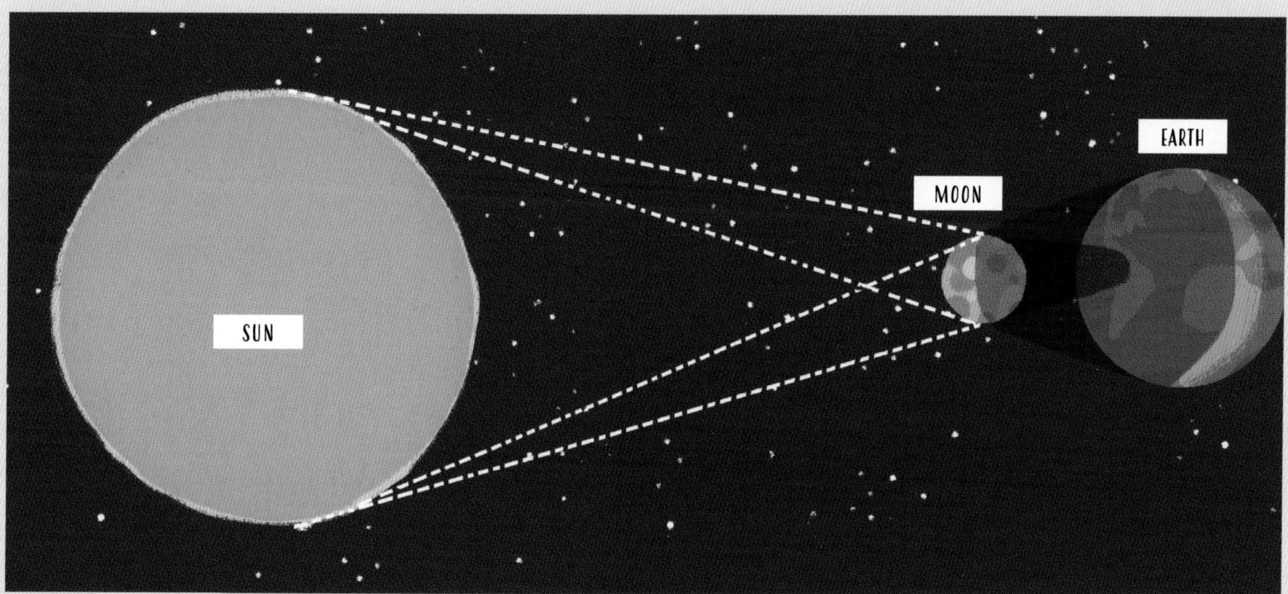

ECLIPSE OF THE SUN

Earth orbits around the Sun. While doing so, our Moon orbits around Earth. Sometimes, the Moon moves directly between Earth and the Sun, and the Moon blocks the Sun's light. This casts a shadow on part of Earth. This is called a solar eclipse. During a total **solar eclipse**, the Sun's outer layer, called the **corona**, can be seen glowing around the outside. **Warning!** The Sun is so bright that it could damage your eyes. Never look at the Sun or an eclipse directly!

OUR HOME PLANET

Rocky planet Earth is the third closest planet to the Sun, about 150 million km (93 million miles) away. It is the only planet known to have life on it—so far.

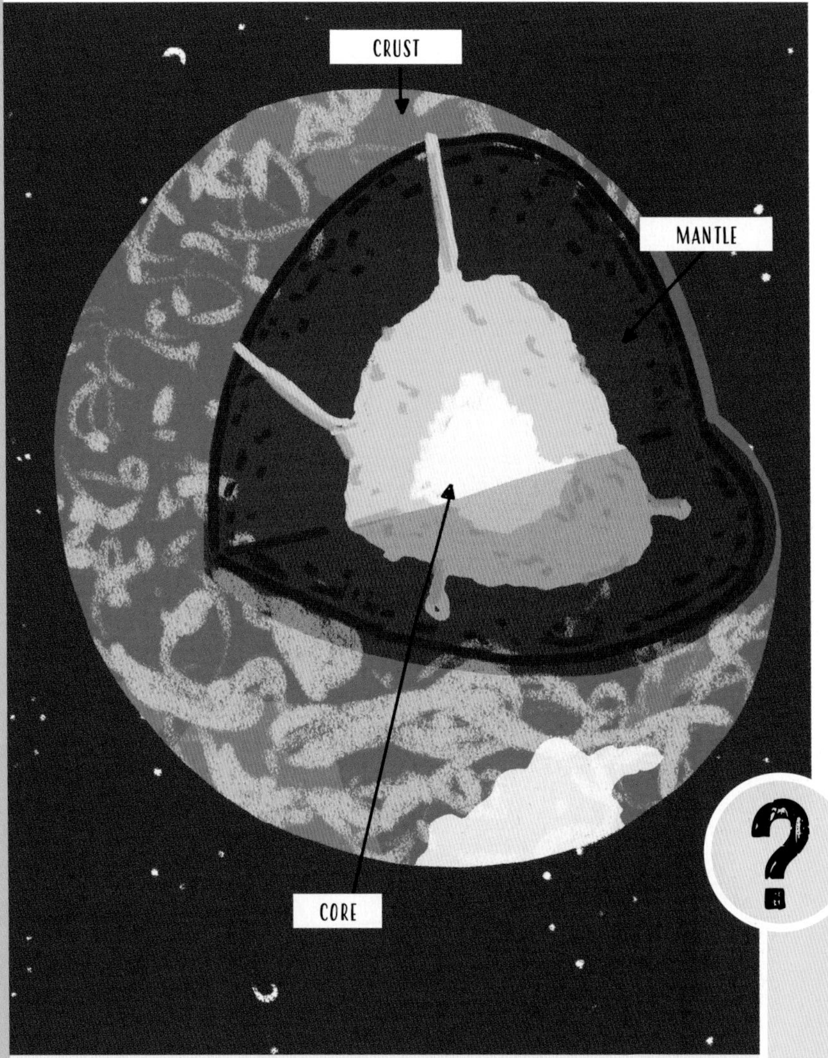

WHAT IS EARTH?

Earth was formed with the Solar System, about 4.6 billion years ago. Gas and dust were pulled together through the force of gravity, forming a ball shape. Dense materials gathered in the **core**, so tightly compacted together that they formed a hot, solid ball. The inner core is about the same temperature as the surface of the Sun. Lighter materials formed the outer rocky **crust**. The thick layer between the crust and core, called the **mantle**, is made of semi-fluid hot magma.

OUT OF CURIOSITY

All the life that we know about in the entire Universe lives only on the thin rocky crust around Earth.

IN A SPIN

Earth spins on its own **axis**—an imaginary line that runs through it from the North Pole to the South Pole. It completes a full rotation on its axis every 24 hours. This is one **day**. As Earth spins, it creates day and night. The areas facing the Sun are in daylight, and daytime, while the areas turned away from the Sun have night.

IN ORBIT

While it is spinning on its axis, Earth also travels through space in **orbit** around the Sun. It completes a full journey around the Sun in just over 365 days. This is one **year**.

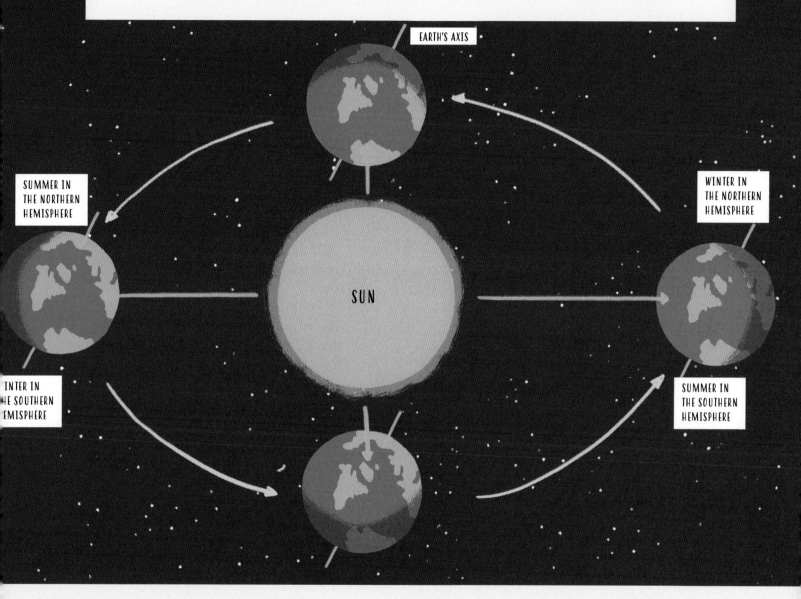

ON A TILT

Earth's axis is tilted at an angle. This is what gives us **seasons**. As Earth travels around in its orbit, different areas spend more or less of each day facing the Sun. There is an invisible line around the middle of Earth called the **equator**. Above the equator is the **Northern Hemisphere**. Below the equator is the **Southern Hemisphere**. When a hemisphere is tilted toward the Sun, it receives more sunlight, and heat, so it is summer. When it is tilted away, less heat energy reaches it, and it is winter. As Earth passes between these positions, it is spring or fall.

Because of the angle of the tilt, regions around the equator get the same strength of the Sun all year round, so they don't have the same changing four seasons.

INFLUENCE OF THE MOON

The Moon and Earth are closely connected. They each have their own gravitational pull that affects the other.

WHAT IS THE MOON?

The **Moon** is a rocky object that circles Earth. Astronomers believe it was formed about 4.5 billion years ago, when a planet about the size of Mars collided with Earth. Bits from the impact were drawn together into a ball shape, trapped by Earth's gravitational pull. Over millions of years, dense materials gathered in the ball's core, and less dense materials moved to the surface. Now, just like Earth, the Moon has a hot metal core and a solid, rocky crust.

THANK YOU, MOON

CHANGING TIDES

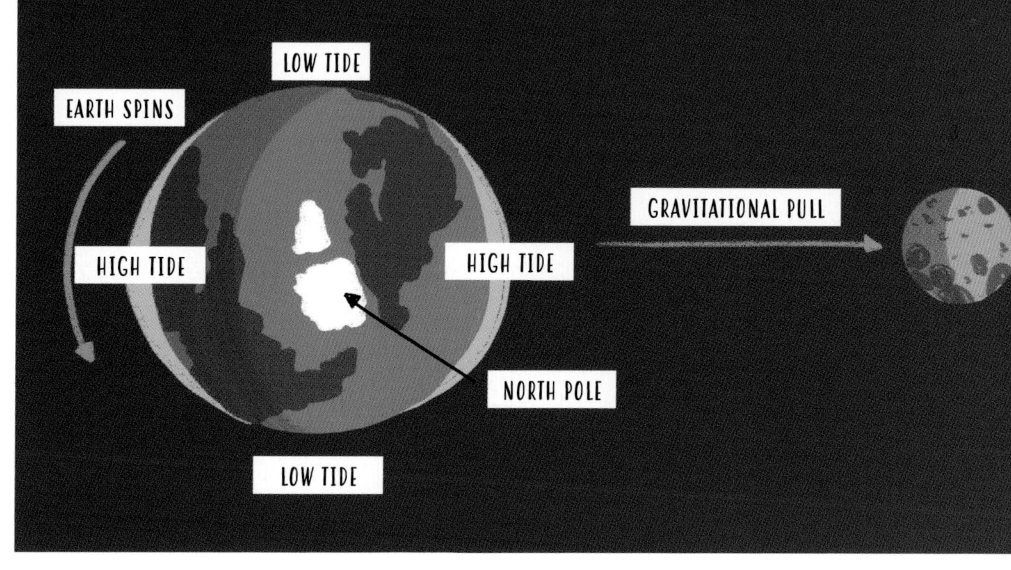

The Moon's gravitational pull generates a **tidal force**. The water on Earth noticeably bulges on the side closest to the Moon, being pulled toward it. Because of Earth's own gravity, the ocean also bulges on the opposite side, farthest from the Moon. These bulges are **high tide**. Earth is almost squeezed, so that two sides bulge, leaving the sections in between flatter—**low tide**. As the Earth spins on its axis, it passes under the two bulges (high tide) and the areas without bulges (low tide). Most coasts experience two high tides and two low tides every day.

The Sun also generates a tidal force, but it isn't as strong because the Sun is so much farther away from Earth than the Moon. When the Sun, Moon, and Earth are all in a line (during a full moon or new moon—see the next page), the gravitational pull is strongest, and the tides are at their highest.

IN BALANCE

As Earth spins on its axis, it has a slight wobble—like a wobbling spinning top. The Moon's gravitational pull helps keep Earth's orbit more stable. Without it, Earth would move back and forth to a greater extent on its axis. Climates and weather would be more extreme. Even our days and seasons wouldn't be the same as we know them now. If the Moon were to disappear, sea creatures that move with the tides and lay eggs in low tides to keep them safe would also feel the effect. Without the Moon, our world could still exist, but it wouldn't be the same.

MOON LANDING

The Moon is the only other place in the Universe (apart from Earth) where human beings have set foot. Humans first stepped on the Moon in 1969. More than 100 robotic spacecraft have also been sent to the Moon to take samples and photos. Eventually, humans hope to set up permanently on the Moon.

LIGHTING THE MOON

The Moon appears to change shape from night to night. For thousands of years, this cycle has guided humans through time. But of course, it is PHYSICS that explains what is happening.

MONTHLY ORBIT

The Moon is Earth's only natural satellite—it is the only natural celestial object that orbits Earth. The Moon takes 27 days to complete a full orbit of Earth. From our perspective, because we are moving too, this appears to be about 29 days. This is a **lunar month**.

SHAPE SHIFTING

The Moon itself does not give off any light. It **reflects** the light of the Sun. The Moon spins on its axis, just like Earth, which means that different parts of the Moon are facing the Sun at different times. When the side of the Moon that faces Earth is fully in sunlight, we see a **full moon**. When the side of the Moon facing Earth is only half lit up, we see a **half moon**. And if the whole Earth-facing side receives no sunlight, we don't see the Moon at all.

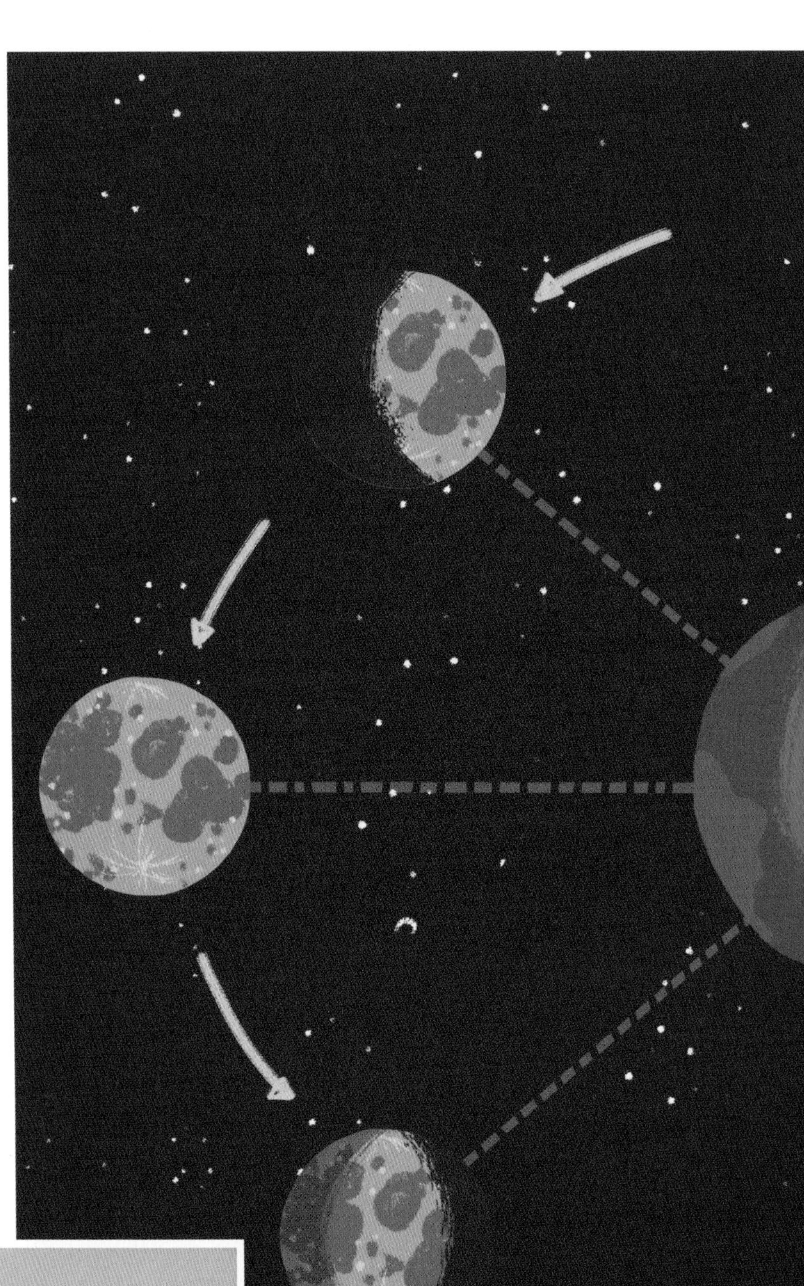

OUT OF CURIOSITY

The Moon spins on its own axis exactly one time in one full orbit of Earth. This means that its near side is always facing us. Humans first saw the far side of the Moon thanks to space travel.

LUNAR ECLIPSE

Just as there can be solar eclipses, there are also **lunar eclipses**. This is when the Moon passes into Earth's shadow, as the Moon, Earth, and Sun line up. In a **total lunar eclipse**, the Moon falls completely in Earth's shadow, and we might see the Moon as a striking shade of red. The shorter blue wavelengths of the Sun's light are reflected outward when they hit the Earth's atmosphere, while the longer wavelengths, such as red, are bent into Earth's shadow. They hit the Moon and make it appear red, similar to a sunset on Earth.

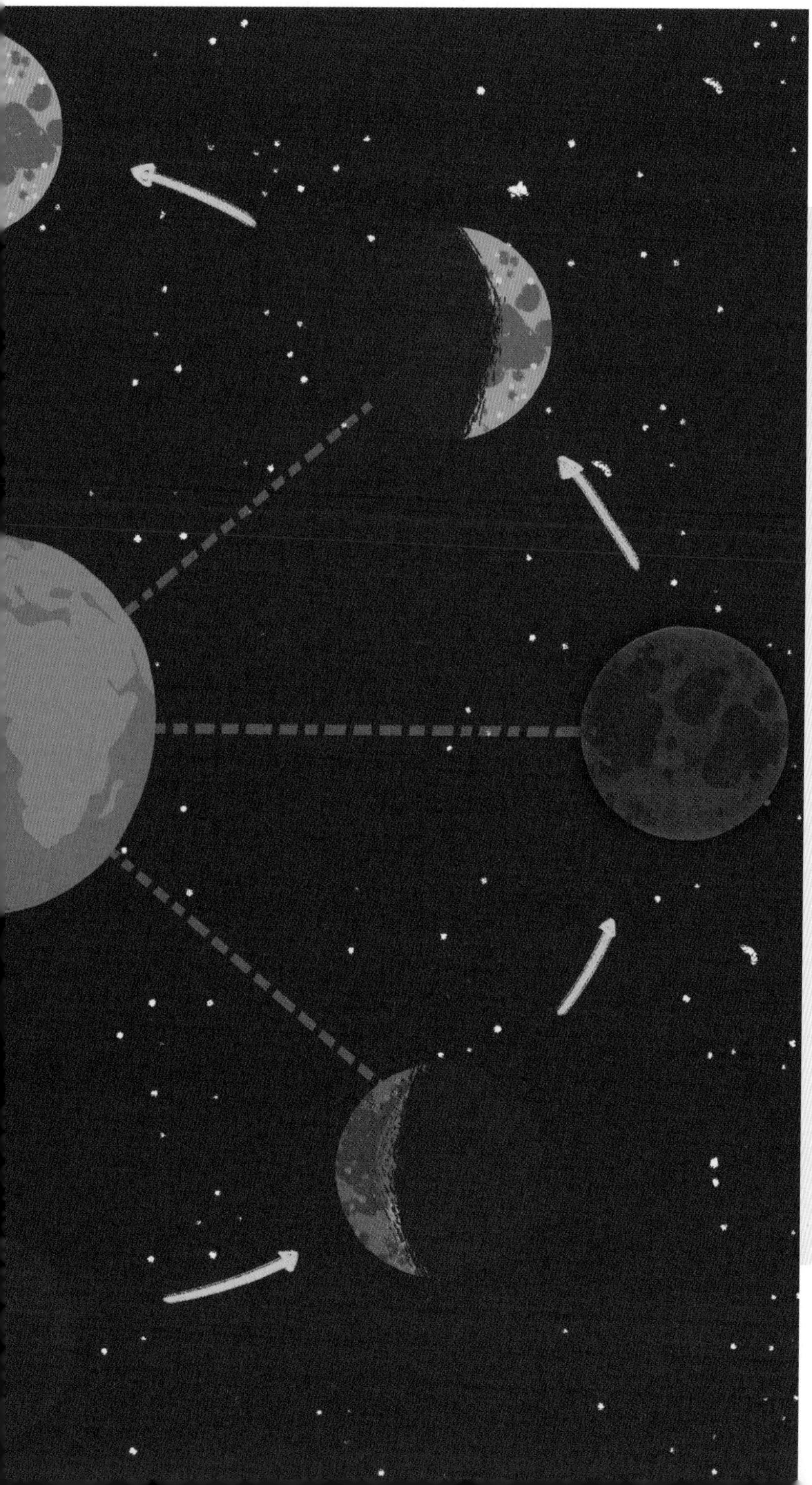

WHY CAN ASTRONAUTS JUMP HIGH ON THE MOON?

Earth is larger than the Moon, with more mass. The greater the mass of an object, the more **gravitational pull** it has. This means that if you jumped on Earth, the Earth's gravity pulls you back down with more force than the Moon's gravity would on the Moon. So, astronauts can jump higher on the Moon than on Earth! The Moon's gravity affects your weight, too. The Moon's gravity is about six times less than it is on Earth, so on the Moon you would weigh about a sixth of your weight on Earth—about the weight of a cat.

INTO DARKNESS

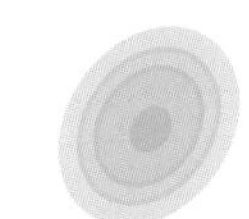

The Universe is full of mysterious things. One of the strangest of all is something that is actually invisible—the **black hole**. We only know black holes exist because of the reaction of other things around them, such as stars and dust.

WHAT IS A BLACK HOLE?

A black hole is an area of space with a gravitational field so strong that nothing can escape it—not even light. Many black holes form when a large star runs out of fuel and dies. The star collapses in on itself into a very tiny space. This leaves an extremely dense area of matter with a very powerful gravitational pull. These black holes are called **stellar black holes** and are scattered throughout the Universe.

Supermassive black holes are found at the middle of every galaxy. Scientists aren't sure how they're formed, but they do know they're HUGE. They can have a mass greater than a million suns. Our own Milky Way spins around a black hole 4 million times more massive than our Sun.

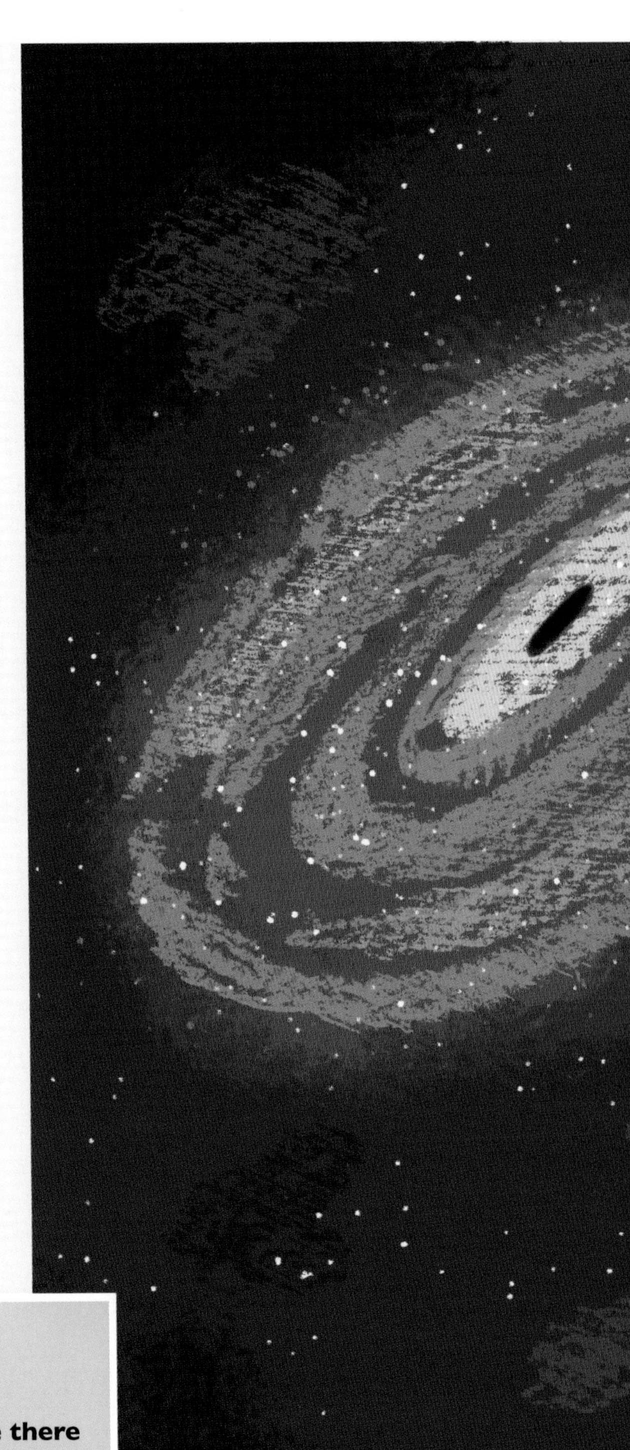

OUT OF CURIOSITY

Earth will never fall into a black hole because there isn't one close enough. And our Sun will never turn into a black hole because it isn't big enough.

POINT OF NO RETURN

This is where things really get strange. As matter flows toward a black hole, pulled in by the black hole's gravity, it speeds up because the pull of gravity becomes stronger. Think of the water rushing along a river toward a waterfall. When it's far away from the cliff, it's moving slow enough for a swimmer to escape. But as it approaches the edge of the waterfall, it speeds up, until there's no way anyone or anything could escape, and the water draws anything in the current over the edge.

The point of no return with a black hole is called the **event horizon**. At this point, matter is moving at the **speed of light**—the fastest thing in the Universe. This means that light itself cannot escape. That is why we call these holes "black."

SEEING THE INVISIBLE

If black holes are black and dark, how can we see them? Scientists know they exist by observing matter around them, close to the event horizon. Stars, gas, dust, and space-time itself are warped. They also become very hot as they are drawn in, so the heat can be detected by super-powerful telescopes. Light rays are bent as they're caught in the gravitational pull. By observing how all these things behave, scientists can try to make sense of these mysterious invisible phenomena.

EXPLORING SPACE

The race is on to travel and explore our Universe. Probes are going farther and farther, and scientists hope to send people farther, too.

IN THE BEGINNING

The first artificial (human-made) satellite was launched into space in 1957. It was a Russian satellite called *Sputnik 1*. A satellite is anything that orbits Earth. *Sputnik 1* orbited the Earth for 22 days, sending back radio signals with information and observations on space and Earth's upper atmosphere.

Sputnik 1 was launched into space on a rocket. It used the law of physics that every action has an **equal and opposite reaction**. As the fuel burned and its explosion pushed down on the ground, the ground pushed back up on the rocket with equal force, sending *Sputnik 1* into space.

FIRSTS IN SPACE

The first person in space was Russian cosmonaut **Yuri Gagarin** in 1961. He orbited Earth in a simple spacecraft and was in space for 108 minutes. In 1965, Russian cosmonaut **Alexei Leonov** performed the first spacewalk—working outside the spaceship. He had to go through a set of doors called an **airlock** to get into space. The pressure in the spaceship is very different from the pressure in space, so the airlock helps to keep the air pressure inside the ship regulated and stops the air that the cosmonaut needs to breathe from rushing out into space. In space, Leonov had a safety line that kept him tied to the ship so he wouldn't float away without gravity to pull him back. He spent about 10 minutes outside in space.

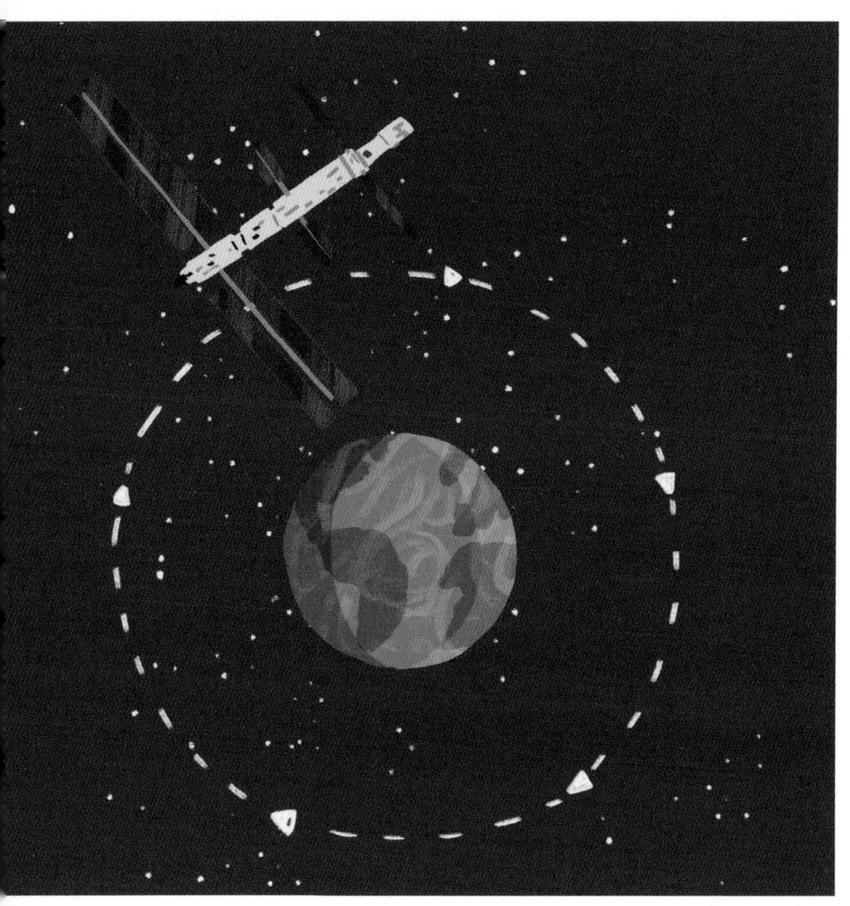

ORBIT OR BEYOND

When a spacecraft travels at just the right speed, it enters into Earth's orbit and begins circling the planet. As the spacecraft leaves Earth, it moves in a curve. It uses a powerful blast that makes it travel very fast, but it is still acted upon by Earth's gravity. If it can travel faster than 40,000 km/h (25,000 mph), called **escape velocity**, it can escape Earth's gravitational pull and begin moving in a straight line toward outer space. If it travels at exactly escape velocity, it will enter **orbit**. It curves all the way around the planet and continues moving in this way. The International Space Station (a spacecraft where astronauts carry out experiments, observations, repairs, and more in space) orbits Earth at this speed.

TRAVEL TODAY

Many spacecraft without people aboard have been sent into space to take pictures and observations in areas much farther than humans can go. These robot explorers are called **probes**. In 2015, for example, the **New Horizons** probe flew past Pluto and gave us the first close-up pictures of the dwarf planet. It went even further to give the first close-up shots of an object in the Kuiper Belt called Arrokoth—the most distant object a probe has been to. In 1977, two probes, **Voyager 1** and **Voyager 2**, were launched. In 2012, Voyager 1 became the first spacecraft to leave our Solar System and travel into interstellar space.

ROBOT EXPLORERS!

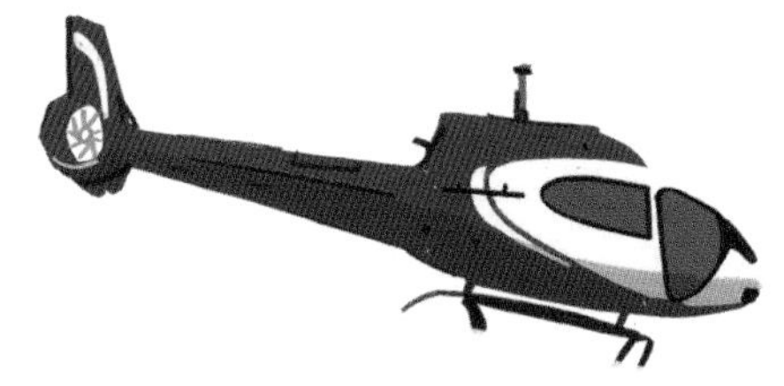

CHAPTER 6

APPLIED PHYSICS: PHYSICS IN ACTION

Look all around you. Bridges, fast cars, skyscrapers—all of these aspects of our lives make use of physics. With a knowledge of forces, energy, atoms, time, and space, people have been able to use physics to build our world.

Applied physics is the practical use of physics—how it's used in the real world. How can bridges support the weight of hundreds of cars? How do cars accelerate so quickly? And how can planes defy gravity to fly? In this chapter we'll answer these questions and many more to put it all together and see physics in action. We'll also take a journey into the future to see what technology might be yet to come. Where will physics take you in your lifetime?

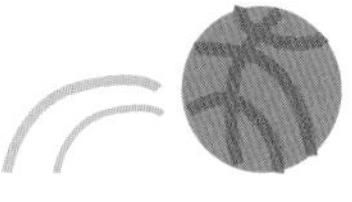

SCIENCE IN SPORTS

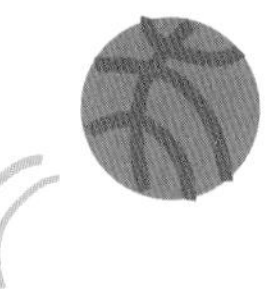

Everyday actions like running, throwing, and kicking a ball use forces and energy to happen. Even the balls themselves owe their designs to physics.

ENERGY TRANSFER

When you play sports, you use stored **chemical energy** in your body. This can be transferred to **kinetic energy** to move your legs to kick a ball, for example. This energy is then transferred to the ball through your leg's push force. The ball gains kinetic energy to fly through the air.

TURBULENCE

When a ball flies through the air, it feels drag from air resistance that slows it down. It also encounters **turbulence** in the form of pockets of air that take kinetic energy from the ball. As a smooth ball flies, it leaves behind it a wide area of turbulent air. Golf balls, though, have their own design. They are designed with evenly spaced small dimples to roughen their surface. These dimples help the air flowing past the ball travel over it more closely, reducing the drag that slows the ball. Dimples help golf balls fly at least three times farther than smooth balls!

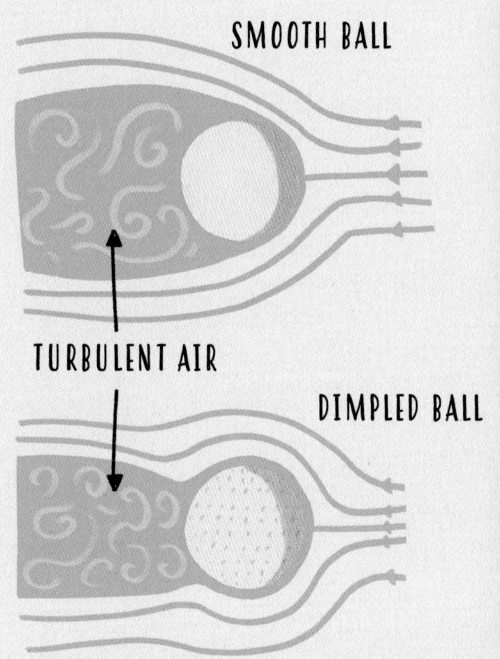

BOUNCE

When a ball hits the ground, the ground pushes back up on it with equal force thanks to **Newton's third law of motion**. This makes the ball bounce. But some balls bounce better than others, and some surfaces give better bounce, too.

A ball travels down to the ground with kinetic energy. The moment the ball hits the ground, it **compresses** and stores the energy as **potential**. When it bounces up again, the stored energy turns back into kinetic energy to keep the ball moving. A basketball is solid on the outside and full of air, so it compresses well to bounce back up high. A softer ball, on the other hand, bends when it hits the ground and barely bounces at all.

A soft bouncing surface, such as the ground, doesn't help with bounce, either. It **absorbs** most of the kinetic energy and takes it from the ball. A hard surface, however, doesn't absorb much energy, so the ball bounces up high again. This is why you'll see basketball players playing on wooden indoor courts and not carpet!

LET'S BOUNCE!

A trampoline uses Newton's third law to help you bounce. The surface is hard but stretchy, and springs allow it to move when you land on it. This means that it doesn't absorb much of your kinetic energy—and it can also push back on you with equal force, so that you bounce as high, or higher, than before!

BUILDING BRIDGES

Bridges allow people, bikes, cars, or trains to cross from one place to another. Early bridges were as simple as logs laid across a narrow river. Since then, they have become more and more elaborate, suited to the space they're crossing and what they will carry.

BALANCING ACT

When designing a bridge, **engineers** must **balance forces** to keep the bridge upright. When the bridge crosses a large area, such as a canyon or body of water, there is nothing to push back up on it. The force of **gravity** pulls down on the bridge, and if there is nothing to balance this, the bridge will collapse. Engineers must balance forces of **tension** (pulling or stretching outward) and **compression** (pushing or squeezing inward). They must also ensure the weight of the load (which includes the bridge itself and anything on it) is balanced and supported.

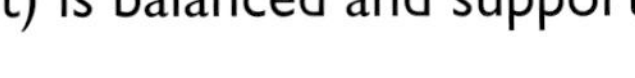

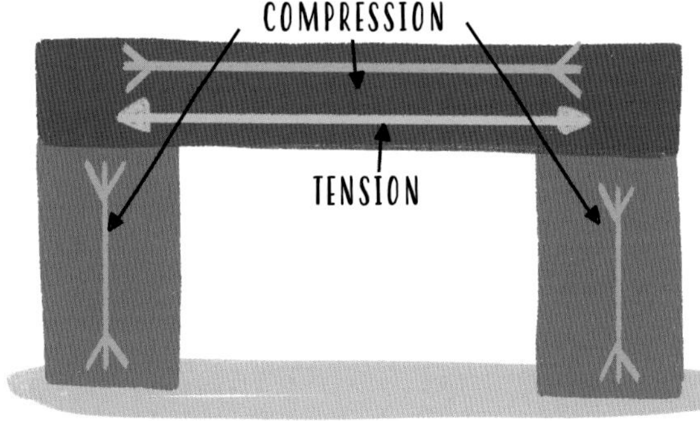

BEAM

The simplest bridge is a **beam bridge**. This is similar to the original log bridge, but it is built higher up. A strong **plank** is supported by **abutments** at each end. A plank sags when an object is on it, subject to both tension and compression forces. The load is transmitted to the abutments, so that they take on some of the compression force. They are squashed down. The longer a beam bridge, the more it will sag in the middle, so simple beam bridges are normally short. Longer, modern beam bridges have repeating reinforcements, such as extra pillars, under them to support the load.

ARCH

Arch bridges use wide supports at each end and a series of **arches** below the plank to share the load. The load pushes down on the ground, and the ground pushes back up with equal force, holding the bridge upright. Arch bridges can span larger distances than beam bridges, but they don't allow all that much clearance underneath.

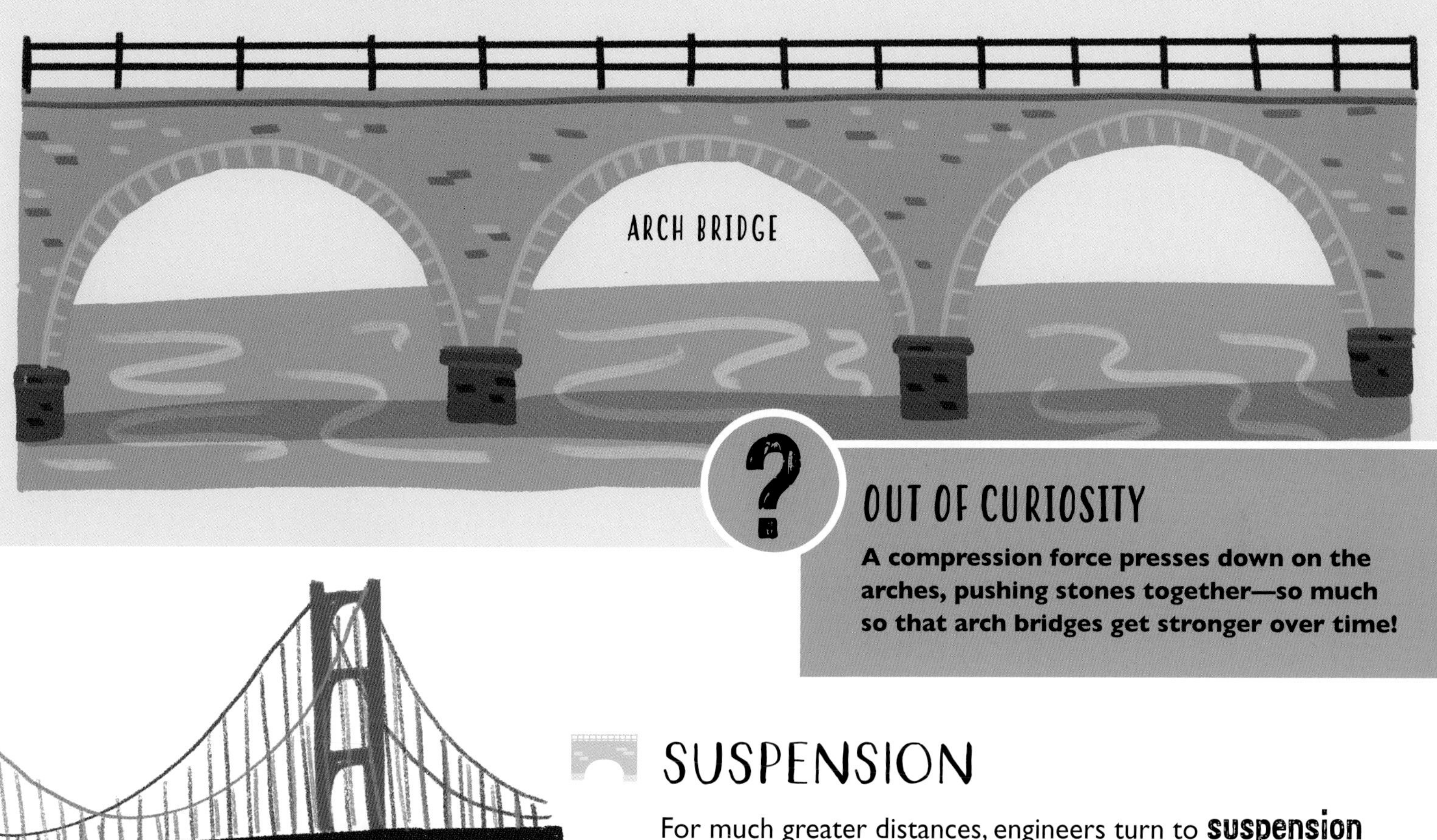

OUT OF CURIOSITY

A compression force presses down on the arches, pushing stones together—so much so that arch bridges get stronger over time!

SUSPENSION BRIDGE

SUSPENSION

For much greater distances, engineers turn to **suspension bridges**. These bridges have girders that support them from below, but they also have very tall towers called **piers** that are used to suspend the bridge from above. Steel **cables** hang from pier to pier, holding up more cables that connect vertically to the crossing to support the load.

CABLE-STAYED

For shorter distances, a shorter **cable-stayed bridge** might be used. It has just one or two towers, and cables connect directly from the tower to the bridge base to hold it up.

CABLE-STAYED BRIDGE

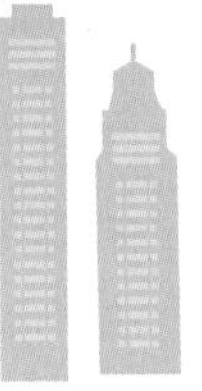

SCRAPING THE SKY

Towering above us and touching the clouds, tall skyscrapers seem to defy gravity.

WHY THE SKY

To gain more building area in a small space, people can build UP. But as they do, they begin fighting **gravity**. Imagine building a tower of blocks. The higher it gets, the harder it is to balance the blocks on top. Any slight imbalance, and the blocks come tumbling down, thanks to Earth's gravity pulling on them.

WEIGHT FOR IT

As skyscrapers become taller, the weight of upper floors can become too much for the lower parts to support, and the buildings can collapse inward. To avoid this, towers must have more weight at the bottom to support the weight above. Pyramids use this principle. They begin with a wide base, and every layer above is smaller than the one below. This means that each layer can support the **combined weight** of the layers above.

BUILDING UP

In a modern city, it isn't practical to have buildings with huge foundations. So engineers and architects turn to new materials to help. In the 1800s, iron and steel became more readily available. Suddenly, architects had new building blocks to work with. Instead of large stones and bricks, they used long, narrow, lightweight **metal beams** that could support large amounts of weight.

ON THE INSIDE

Inside every fancy skyscraper is its **steel skeleton**. Vertical metal beams provide support between floors, which are created from horizontal beams. Many tall buildings use diagonal beams to provide extra support, too. All the weight is transferred to the vertical posts. The force of gravity presses down through the vertical posts onto a support structure at the base. Deep foundations are anchored to bedrock in the Earth to support the structure above.

SWAYING IN THE BREEZE

As skyscrapers rise higher, they are more open to the force of the **wind**. They are able to sway back and forth without falling down—but the people inside might notice! To avoid noticeable movement, the steel skeleton is securely connected at each intersecting point of beams. Especially tall buildings also have extra reinforcement down their middles to create super-strong cores that will not only resist wind, but also earthquake damage. Skyscrapers also have dampers and shock absorbers to disperse energy. New technologies and even computer applications are continuously being developed to manage wind shift.

THE SEARCH FOR SPEED

Many people use cars to get around, and to carry shopping and luggage—while others use them for SPEED.

NEED FOR SPEED

Speed is how fast something moves from one place to the next. In physics, we also talk about **velocity**. This is how fast something moves **in a particular direction**. Cars moving in different directions can have the same speed, but different velocities.

Speed is relative. Even when you feel that you're sitting still, the Earth is spinning, and soaring around the Sun, too. Because of this, speed is hard to feel. But **acceleration** is much more noticeable. Acceleration is any **change** in velocity. This means any change in your speed as you travel in one direction. Think about when you're moving in a car or train, and the driver stops suddenly. Your body jolts forward! On the other hand, if a car speeds up really fast, you're pushed back into your seat. And if the vehicle turns sharply, your body feels pushed to the side.

These feelings are because of **Newton's first law** of motion. Your body continues to move in the same direction and speed that it was going. This is called **inertia**.

IT'S THE LAW!

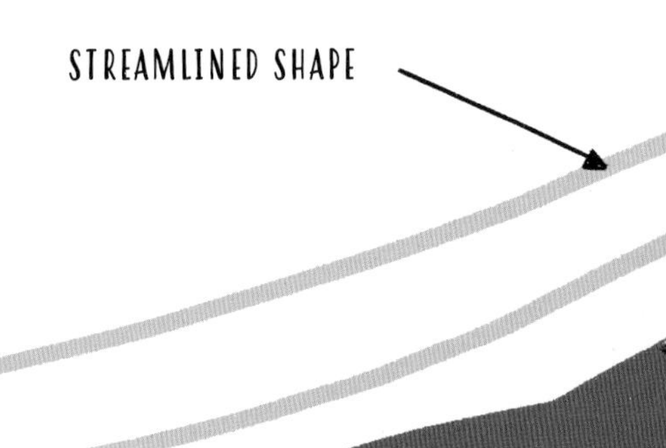

G FORCE

When the car stops suddenly, your body keeps moving in the same forward motion that it was going, until it is halted by the seatbelt. When the car turns sharply to one side, your body continues in the other direction that it had been going, so it feels like you're pushed that way. The feeling of inertia trying to keep you moving is called **g force** (the g stands for gravity). Race car drivers experience strong g force because they are going so fast.

AIR RESISTANCE

How fast something goes depends on how heavy that object is, how much power it has, and the **friction** it is up against. Cars can travel faster on smooth roads than on bumpy ones. The smooth surface means there is less friction between the wheels and the road to slow down the car. Friction can also come from **air resistance**. The more surface area an object has, the more air can hit it and slow it down. As vehicles move faster, they experience even more air resistance. Race cars are designed with smooth, **streamlined** shapes that direct the air up and around the car to reduce any drag. Many race cars also have a spoiler, or wing, at the back to push them down so they don't lift off the ground at high speeds!

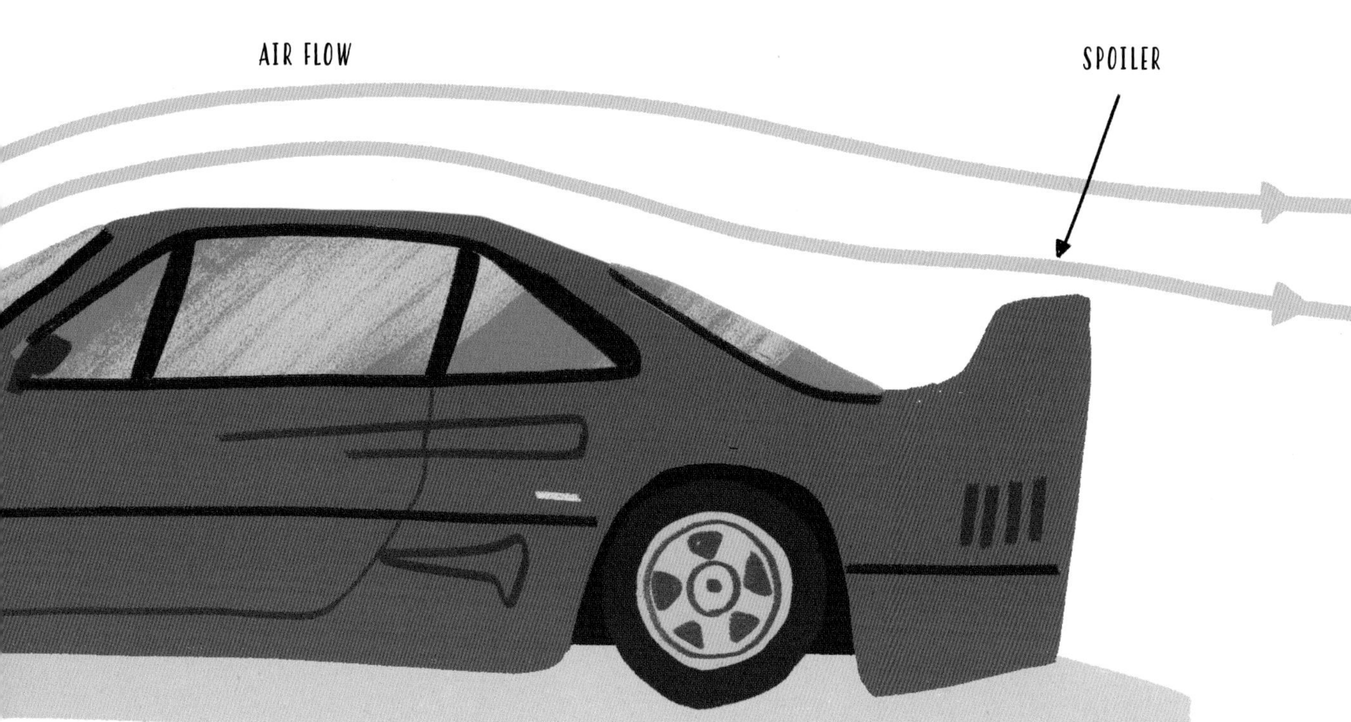

FINDING FLIGHT

Human flight began over 200 years ago with the invention of hot air balloons and gliders. But it wasn't until the 1900s that engine-powered flights took off, changing everything. Suddenly people could travel faster and farther than ever before.

LEONARDO DA VINCI

Hundreds of years before the first planes took flight, Italian inventor and artist **Leonardo da Vinci** sketched plans for aircraft. Born in 1452, he was a part of the Renaissance, a period full of discoveries and cultural curiosity. He drew many designs for flying machines, including wings for humans. His ideas were never built and weren't discovered until after he died.

DRAG

FIGHTING FORCES

When an object flies, there are four main forces that act on it.

Drag: Drag pushes on an aircraft in the opposite direction to its travel and tries to slow it down. It is the same as air resistance. As the aircraft moves faster through the air, drag increases. Planes are designed with streamlined, smooth shapes to direct air around them and reduce drag.

Lift: Lift is the opposite of gravity and is provided by air. It pushes an object upward and holds it in the air. As a plane flies fast through the sky, the air is directed around the plane's wings. The wings are rounded on top so that air moves faster across the top than the bottom. This faster air has lower pressure than the slower-moving air under the wing, so the wing feels an upward push from below.

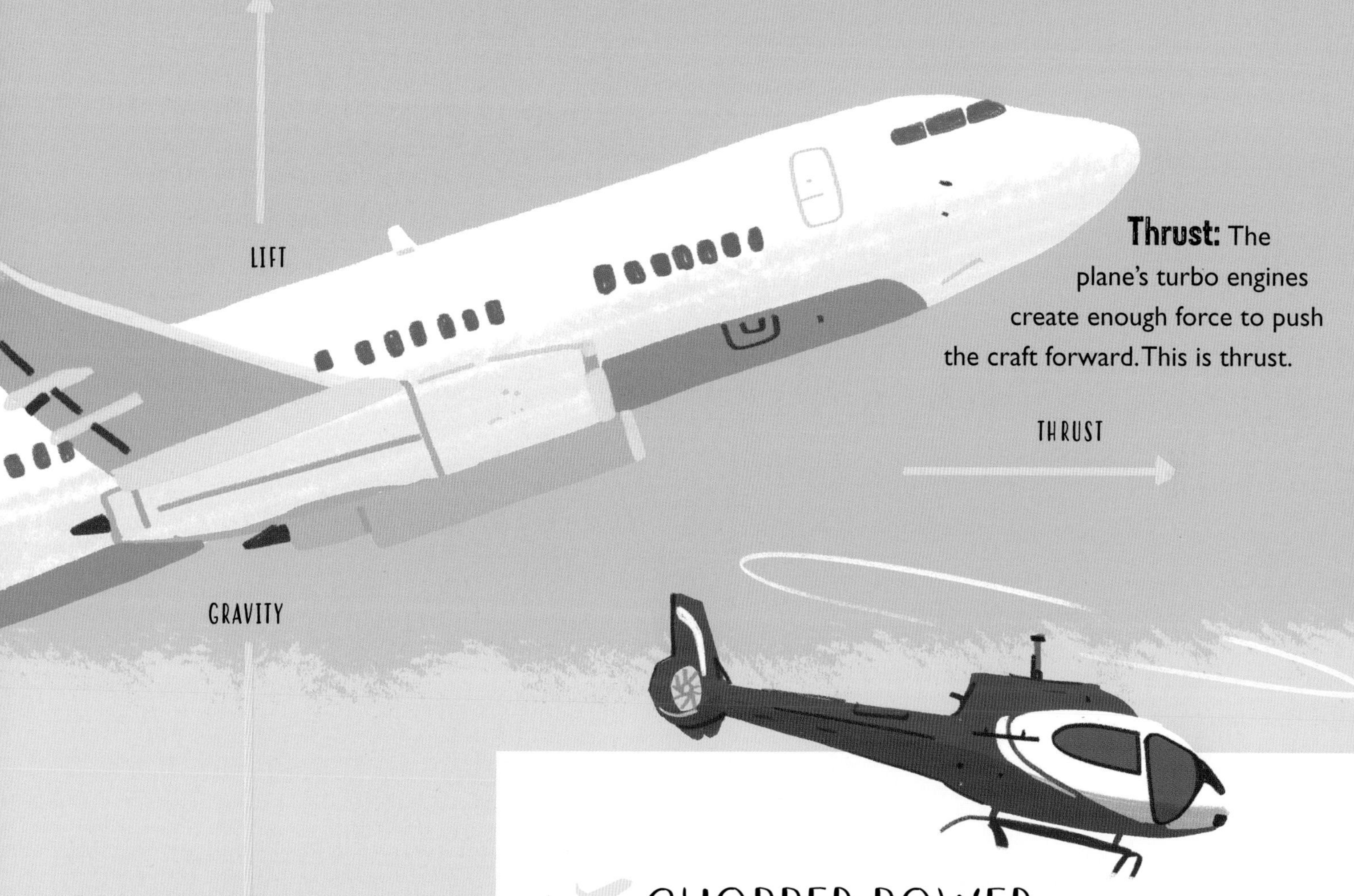

Thrust: The plane's turbo engines create enough force to push the craft forward. This is thrust.

Gravity: To get up in the sky, an object must overcome gravity. Earth's gravity pulls the aircraft down toward the ground. Planes and helicopters use powerful engines, along with their wings and rotors, to overcome this.

CHOPPER POWER

A **helicopter** is acted upon by the same four forces as a plane, but it flies in its own way. To create lift, the helicopter has **rotors**. These are blades that spin very fast. Just like the plane's wings, they are curved at the top. This creates a faster air flow at the top and higher pressure below, which pushes upward. Because it creates its own lift, a helicopter can take off directly upward, without needing a runway like a plane. When all four forces are balanced, helicopters can hover in the air. They can even fly backward!

BUOYANT BOATS

With their heavy metal frames, you'd think that boats would sink to the bottom of the sea. But in fact, they can float if their designers have a good grasp of physics!

ARCHIMEDES

Born in 287 BCE, Archimedes was a famous inventor and mathematician. His **Archimedes' Principle** helps us understand how boats float. He discovered that when an object is placed in water, that object **displaces** the water—moves it out of the way. For example, when you get in a bathtub, the water level rises. This is because your body takes its place and pushes the water upward. Archimedes went on to say that the upward force that acts on an object in water is equal to the weight of the water displaced by that object. This force is called **buoyancy**.

TO FLOAT OR TO SINK

Following on from Archimedes' Principle, we know that an object will **sink** if it weighs more than the water it displaces because the buoyant force will not be strong enough to push it up. The object will **float** if it weighs less or the same than the water it displaces. This means that to float, a boat must weigh less than the water it sits on. But how can it when it is built of heavy materials? The answer lies in something that weighs close to nothing.

Boats are full of **air**. They are built to be large vessels that take up space on the water, but much of their body is hollowed out and filled with air. This means that the space they take up on the water weighs less than or the same as the huge amount of water they displace. Water pushes up on the ship with a greater force than the weight of the ship and keeps it afloat.

OUT OF CURIOSITY

The world's largest cruise ships today are as tall as 16-level buildings and longer than three and a half football fields laid end to end. They can carry nearly half a million people—and still float!

GOING DOWN

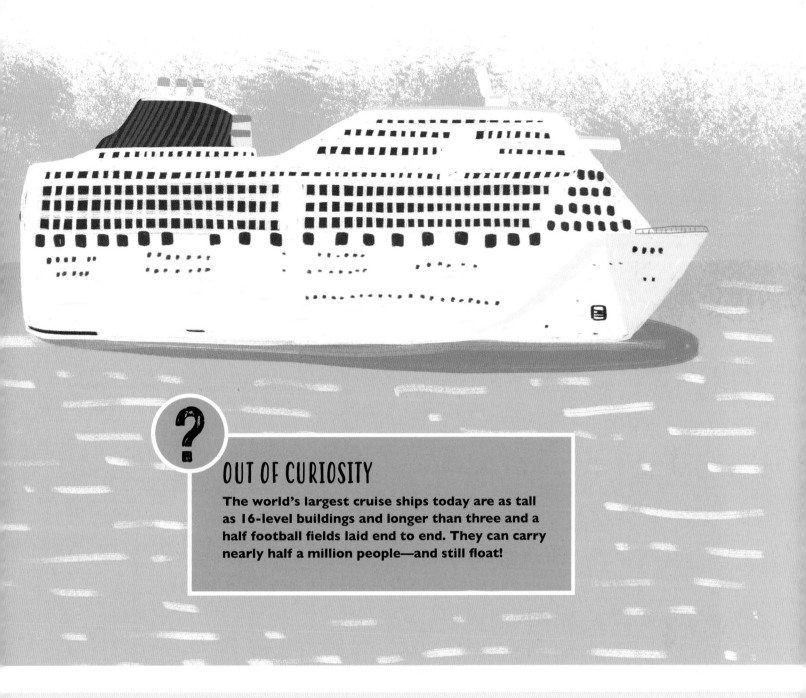

The *Titanic* is a ship that famously and tragically sank in 1912. As it sailed across the sea, it struck an iceberg below the surface. The iceberg tore holes in the ship's shell, letting water in. Water took the place of the air inside, and soon the ship became much heavier—so heavy that it could no longer float. The ship was no longer buoyant and eventually sank to the bottom of the sea.

OFF THE RAILS

The physics of magnets has been used to create a friction-defying type of train—one that hovers above the tracks.

TRAINS AND TRACKS

Rails have been around for hundreds of years, carrying carts and later trains along tracks. Trains today have **engines** that power them along. Most high-speed and inner-city trains use **electricity**, too. Motors turn the train wheels, which grip the track and move the train along.

MAGNETIC LEVITATION

Maglev trains (short for magnetic levitation) are different. Instead of sitting on tracks, they hover above them. Instead of using fuel for power, they use **electromagnetism**.

We know that opposite poles on a magnet attract, and similar poles repel. The bottom of the maglev train is fitted with large magnets, and magnetic coils are wound around the track, too. A current of electricity flows through the coils to create electromagnets. These powerful magnets repel, pushing the train away so that it levitates above the track. Electricity is used to change the magnets' **polarity** so that the magnets in front of the train are attracting, to pull the train forward, and the magnets behind the train are repelling, to add extra push.

HOW DOES IT STOP?

A maglev train does not have brakes like other trains. So how does it stop? Just as it moves forward with electromagnetism, it stops using magnetism too! The electric current running through the coils is reversed, so that the polarity is **reversed**, too. Now, the magnets **repel** at the front of the train, pushing on it, and **attract** at the back, pulling on the train to slow it down to a stop.

Magnets repelling to keep the train from touching the sides of the track.
Magnets repelling to lift and move the train.
TRACK

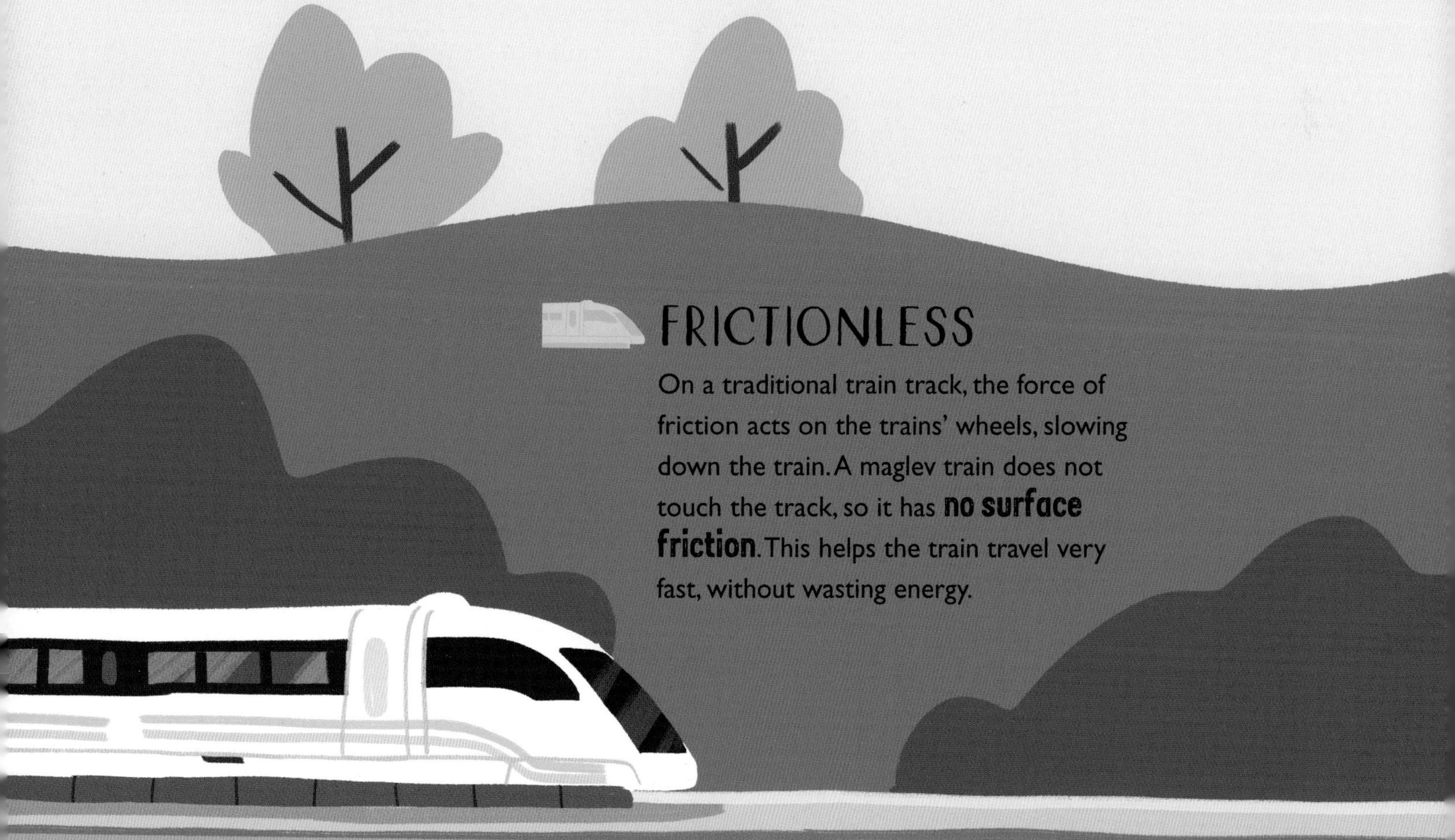

FRICTIONLESS

On a traditional train track, the force of friction acts on the trains' wheels, slowing down the train. A maglev train does not touch the track, so it has **no surface friction**. This helps the train travel very fast, without wasting energy.

AIR RESISTANCE

Although there is no friction from the tracks, the train still experiences friction from **air resistance.** As it travels quickly, air resistance increases. Air pushes on the train and slows it down. The train is designed with a smooth, streamlined body to direct air around it and travel quickly through air.

NEW TECHNOLOGIES

Physicists are constantly pushing the boundaries to find new ways to put physics to work in our world.

NANOTECH

Nanotechnology is science at the **nanoscale** level. One **nanometer** (nm) is a BILLIONTH of a meter. Just one human hair can be 100,000 nm wide. That's extremely small! The nanoscale includes objects that are just 1 to 100 nm in size. This is normally working at the atomic or molecular level—working with atoms and molecules. Scientists use special microscopes to see and control matter at the nanoscale. Because they are working with atoms, the building blocks of matter, they can strengthen or manipulate materials at their bottom level. For example, lighter materials are being developed for cars, aircraft, boats, and even spacecraft. These would reduce the fuel needed, saving on cost and planet-unfriendly emissions.

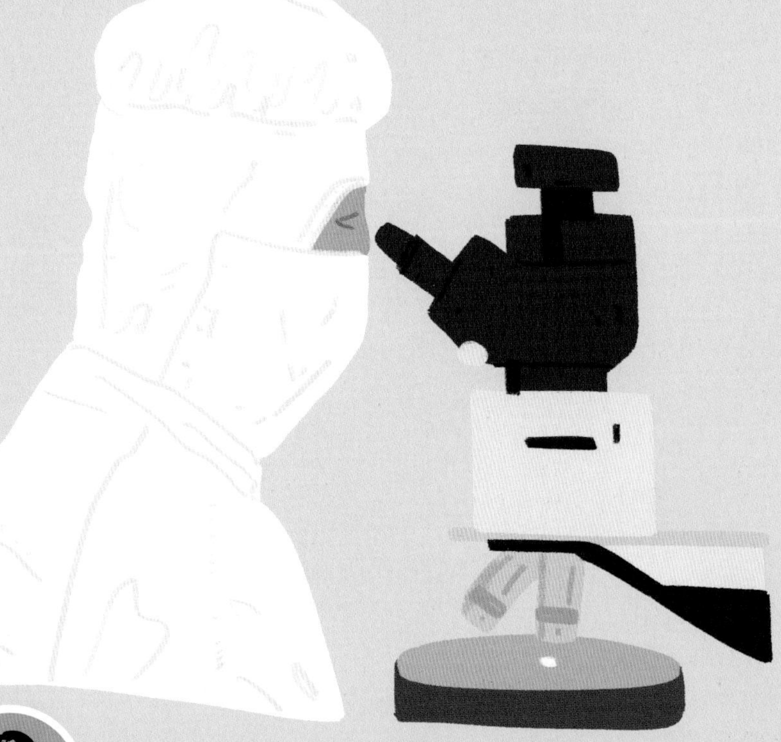

OUT OF CURIOSITY

Your fingernails grow about 1 nm per second! That's about 86,400 nm, or less than a tenth of a mm, per day, but that's still so small that you don't even notice.

DRIVERLESS CARS

We often think of cars and drivers as going hand in hand. But do they need to? **Self-driving**, or autonomous, driverless cars are cars that can drive themselves! Most of them use sensors to map their surroundings as they go. The car can then brake, steer, or accelerate in response. This technology could help more people travel, but then that could cause an increase in fuel emissions, unless the cars are electrified or use alternative fuel. A road where all cars have no drivers is a long way off, but it is certainly on people's minds.

MEDICINE

High-frequency sound waves are used to create images of objects inside the body, such as developing babies or soft tissue. Ultrasonic sound waves reflect off the tissue to create a picture on a screen. Traditionally, ultrasound images have been 2D, flat pictures. More recently, 3D ultrasounds have been possible, with sound waves beamed in at an angle to provide an image with depth. And now, technologists can even add a **fourth dimension**—time. Ultrasound scans in 4D show the picture in real time, as a video scan. New technologies in ultrasound also include **sonoelastography**. This technique involves testing how **elastic** the tissue is to determine its stiffness, which can potentially help identify cancers or muscular-skeletal concerns.

FUTURISTIC PHYSICS 

Scientists never stop asking questions. Sometimes ideas might seem too futuristic to be possible, but eventually they could become the reality of the present!

INNOVATIVE ENERGY

With some sources of energy running out, and others expensive to harness, scientists are always on the quest to find new ways to generate electricity.

Magma power: Geothermal energy, which is already in use, is energy harnessed from heat underground—water is piped down and heated by hot rocks, which turn it to steam that rises and turns turbines. Scientists have now discovered that if they dig even deeper by volcanoes, magma could heat the water to much higher temperatures. This **magma power** would generate up to **10 times** more energy than normal geothermal power. It is being investigated and tested in volcanic places like Iceland.

POWER STATION BY VOLCANIC LAND

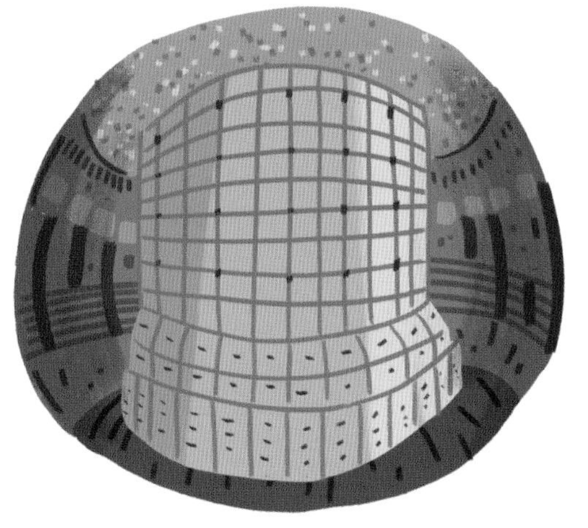

FUSION REACTOR

Fusion reactor: The Sun releases energy through nuclear fusion. Hydrogen nuclei join together and create helium atoms, releasing a huge amount of energy in the process. A **fusion reactor** is intended to be a device that attempts to recreate this process. A ring-shaped tube contains hydrogen, which is heated to temperatures as hot as the Sun. The nuclei fuse together and release enormous amounts of energy. This Earth-friendly technology could be life-changing, but it is very expensive and difficult to build, so it is still many years away.

DYSON SWARM

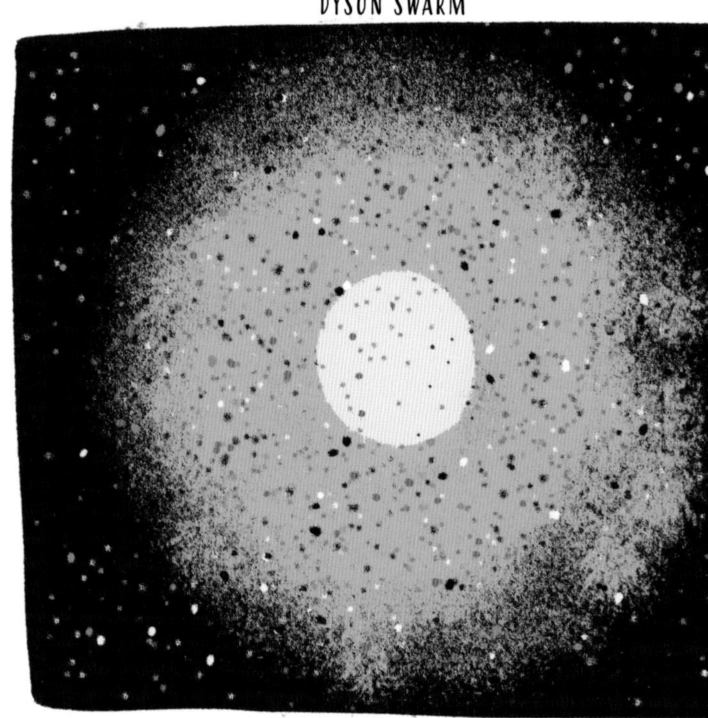

Dyson sphere: A fusion reactor attempts to reproduce the power of the Sun. A **Dyson sphere** would attempt to actually capture energy from a star. It is an idea that you could put a mega structure the shape of a sphere and the size of the Solar System around a star to collect its heat and light energy. It would be a hollow structure that would surround the entire solar system. A Dyson Swarm could be another possibility, surrounding a star, or the Sun, with thousands of mirrors or solar panels to harness its power. These are all ideas at the moment and not yet possible to build!

TRAVEL IN TIME

In science fiction stories, people have long explored the idea of time travel. Some physicists ponder this as well. Einstein introduced the idea that the faster you move, the slower time goes. So, in space, as you move faster and faster, time slows down. Clocks on the International Space Station, which orbits the Earth, do indeed show a very minimal decrease in time passed compared to clocks on Earth. In theory then, if you came back to Earth after exploring space at nearly the speed of light, you would return younger than everyone else—like coming back in the future! Scientists are also exploring theories of wormholes in space or particles that can move backward. But how safe would it be to travel in this way? Could it change a timeline to meet a past or future version of yourself? Should we time travel at all? What do you think?

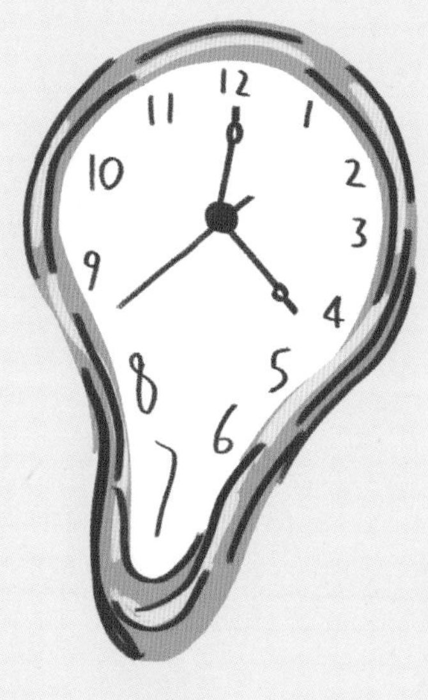

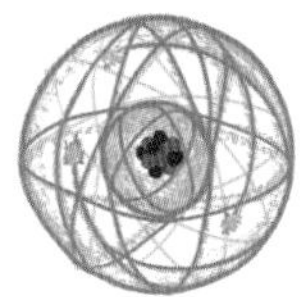

GLOSSARY

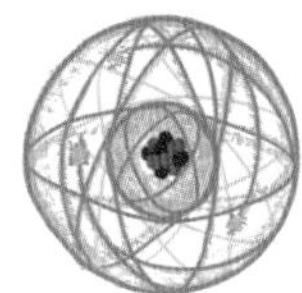

acceleration: How quickly an object speeds up.

acoustics: Relating to sound and hearing.

aerodynamic: Having a shape that allows an object to pass swiftly through air, reducing air resistance.

air resistance: The force that acts on an object as it moves through air.

amplitude: The highest point of a wave, measured from the middle.

atom: A tiny particle that is the basic unit of matter.

attract: To cause to draw together.

biomass: Plant or animal matter used as fuel.

buoyant: Able to stay afloat or rise to the surface.

celestial: In or relating to the sky or space.

chemical bond: A force holding atoms together.

conduction: The process of heat, sound, or electricity being transmitted through a substance.

convection: The process of heat being transferred through a liquid or gas due to moving currents created by hot material rising and cold material sinking.

cosmonaut: An astronaut from Russia.

deceleration: How quickly an object slows down.

dense: When matter is closely compacted together.

drag: The force of resistance experienced by an object moving through a liquid or gas, such as water or air.

electricity: Energy from the movement of charged particles.

electron: A particle with a negative charge, found in an atom.

emit: To produce and let out.

energy: Something that can do work and make things happen.

engineer: A person who designs, builds, or maintains machines and engines.

force: A push or a pull that can change the movement or shape of an object.

fossil fuel: A fuel, such as coal or gas, made from the remains of organisms that died millions of years ago.

foundation: The lowest level of a building, which bears the load. It is often underground.

frequency: The number of waves of a vibration in a second.

galaxy: A group of stars, gas, and dust held together by gravity.

generator: A machine that can convert kinetic energy into electricity.

gravity: A force that attracts objects toward each other.

harness: To control and use, such as harnessing solar power to produce electricity.

insulator: A substance that does not easily conduct heat, sound, or electricity.

kinetic: Relating to motion.

magnetism: An invisible force between some materials, causing them to attract or repel.

magnify: To make something appear larger than it is.

mass: The amount of matter an object contains.

matter: Something that has mass and takes up space. What all things are made of.

molecule: A group of atoms bonded together.

nebula: A cloud of gas and dust in space.

neutron: A particle with no electric charge, found in the nucleus of most atoms

non-renewable energy: Energy from sources that cannot be easily replaced, such as oil.

nuclear fusion: A reaction when nuclei join together to form a heavier nucleus, releasing energy in the process.

nucleus: The solid central part of an atom, made up of protons and neutrons.

optics: The study of sight and how light behaves.

orbit: To move around a star or planet in a regular, repeated path.

particle: A basic unit of matter, such as an atom or molecule, that makes up substances.

photon: A tiny packet of energy, such as a particle of light.

pitch: The highness or lowness of a sound.

pressure: The amount of pushing force acting over an area.

probe: An unmanned spacecraft sent into space to explore and send data and photos back to Earth.

proton: A particle with a positive charge, found in an atom's nucleus.

radiation: Energy that travels as electromagnetic rays.

reflect: To bounce back without absorbing.

refract: When a ray of light bends as it passes from one substance to another.

renewable energy: Energy from sources that won't run out, such as solar or wind power.

repel: To force apart.

streamlined: Having a shape that reduces air or water resistance.

thrust: A forward push, such as from a jet or rocket engine.

tide: The rise and fall of the ocean.

upthrust: The upward force that a liquid or gas exerts on an object.

vacuum: A space without any matter.

velocity: How fast something moves in a specific direction.

vibration: A back and forth shaking of an object, substance, or wave.

water resistance: The force that acts on an object as it moves through water.

wavelength: The distance between one crest of a wave and the crest next to it.

weight: The force that acts on an object's mass due to gravity.

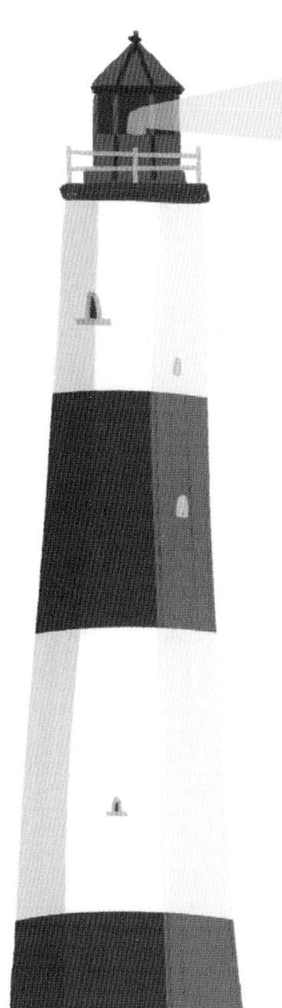

INDEX

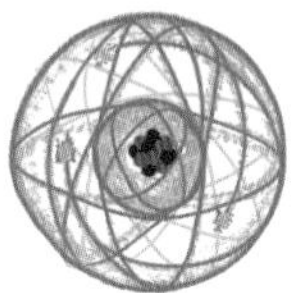